Tides of Change:
Mitigating Plastic Pollution in Small Island Developing States

OrangeBooks Publication

1st Floor, Rajhans Arcade, Mall Road, Kohka, Bhilai, Chhattisgarh 490020

Website: www.orangebooks.in

© **Copyright, 2024, Author**

All rights reserved. No part of this book may be reproduced, stored in a retrieval system, or transmitted, in any form by any means, electronic, mechanical, magnetic, optical, chemical, manual, photocopying, recording or otherwise, without the prior written consent of its writer.

First Edition, 2024

ISBN: 978-93-5621-607-5

TIDES OF CHANGE

MITIGATING PLASTIC POLLUTION IN SMALL ISLAND DEVELOPING STATES

DR. CHIRAG BHIMANI

OrangeBooks Publication
www.orangebooks.in

Table of Contents

Foreword ix
Preface xiii
About the Book xvii

Chapter 1 - Introduction 1

Introduction 3
    Understanding the Scope of Plastic Pollution 4
    The Vulnerability of Small Island Developing States (SIDS) 5

Chapter 2 - The Impact of Plastic Pollution on SIDS 9

The Impact of Plastic Pollution on SIDS 11
    Ecological Consequences 12
    Economic Implications 16
    Social and Cultural Effects 20

Chapter 3 - Root Causes of Plastic Pollution 27

Root Causes of Plastic Pollution 29
    Consumer Behaviour 30
    Inadequate Waste Management Systems 35
    Single-Use Plastics and Packaging 41

Chapter 4 - Policy and Legislative Frameworks 49

Policy and Legislative Frameworks 51
- International Agreements and Protocols 52
- National Strategies and Initiatives 56
- Regional Collaboration Efforts 65

Chapter 5 - Innovative Solutions 73

Innovative Solutions 75
- Waste Reduction and Recycling Programs 76
- Sustainable Alternatives to Plastic 81
- Community Engagement and Education 87

Chapter 6 - Case Studies from SIDS 95

Case Studies from SIDS 97
- Success Stories 97
- Ongoing Challenges 102
- Lessons Learned 108

Chapter 7 The Role of Technology 115

The Role of Technology 117
- Monitoring and Detection Systems 118
- Ocean Cleanup Technologies 124
- Data-driven Approaches 125

Chapter 8 Building Resilience 129

Building Resilience 131
- Adapting to Climate Change 132
- Integrating Plastic Pollution Mitigation into Sustainable Development Goals 139

Chapter 9 Partnerships and Collaborations.................................... 149

Partnerships and Collaborations 151
Governmental and Non-Governmental Organizations (NGOs) 152

Private Sector Engagement 159

Civil Society and Community Participation 165

Chapter 10 - Future Perspectives 173

Future Perspectives 175
Emerging Trends and Technologies 176
Long-term Strategies for SIDS 182
The Global Fight Against Plastic Pollution 191

Chapter 11 - Conclusion 201

Conclusion 203
The Urgency of Action 204
Hope for a Sustainable Future 210

Epilogue - A Call to Action 219

Glossary of Terms 225

References 233

Further Reading 243

Notes 251

Foreword

In the vast expanse of our oceans lies a challenge that transcends borders, cultures, and ideologies: plastic pollution. Its insidious grip on marine ecosystems threatens not only the health of our planet but also the livelihoods and well-being of millions of people, particularly those in Small Island Developing States (SIDS).

Tides of Change: Mitigating Plastic Pollution in Small Island Developing States is a timely and vital contribution to the global conversation on environmental sustainability. In this groundbreaking book, readers are invited on a journey of discovery– a journey that traverses the turquoise waters of SIDS, confronts the stark realities of plastic pollution, and embraces the promise of innovation and collaboration.

Through meticulous research, insightful analysis, and compelling storytelling, the authors illuminate the complex interplay of factors driving plastic pollution in SIDS–from consumer behaviour and inadequate waste management systems to the omnipresence of single-use plastics. They shine a spotlight on the profound impacts of plastic pollution on the environment, economy, and social fabric of SIDS communities, underscoring the urgency of action.

Yet, amidst these challenges, **Tides of Change** offers a beacon of hope. It showcases the resilience, ingenuity, and determination of SIDS in tackling plastic pollution head-on. From pioneering policy and legislative frameworks to fostering grassroots initiatives and embracing cutting-edge technologies, SIDS are leading the charge towards a plastic-free future.

This book is not merely a call to action; it is a call to solidarity. It reminds us that the fight against plastic pollution knows no boundaries and that we must stand together as global citizens to safeguard our oceans and preserve the rich biodiversity and cultural heritage of SIDS for generations to come.

As you embark on this transformative journey through the pages of **Tides of Change**, may you be inspired to join the ranks of change-makers and champions of sustainability around the world. May you heed the call of the oceans, whose tides of change beckon us to rise to the challenge and chart a course towards a brighter, cleaner, and more resilient future.

Ibrahim Nizam
Brand Strategist &
Hospitality Consultant
Male, Maldives

Preface

In the vast expanse of our oceans, a silent threat lurks beneath the surface, imperilling the delicate ecosystems and vibrant communities of Small Island Developing States (SIDS). Plastic pollution, with its insidious reach and enduring presence, poses a formidable challenge to the very essence of life in these island nations.

Tides of Change: Mitigating Plastic Pollution in Small Island Developing States is a testament to the urgency of action and the power of collective endeavour in confronting this shared threat. Within these pages, readers will embark on a journey of discovery, guided by insights from scientists, policymakers, activists, and community leaders who are at the forefront of the battle against plastic pollution.

As the author of this book, I am humbled by the magnitude of the challenge before me and inspired by the resilience and determination of those who refuse to surrender to despair. Through meticulous research, thoughtful analysis, and impassioned advocacy, I have sought to illuminate the complex interplay of forces driving plastic pollution in SIDS and chart a course towards a more sustainable and equitable future.

From the teeming coral reefs of the Caribbean to the remote atolls of the Pacific, the stories contained herein offer glimpses into both the devastation wrought by plastic pollution and the rays of hope that pierce through the darkness. I invite readers to bear witness to the ingenuity of communities devising innovative solutions, the steadfastness of leaders forging bold policies, and the compassion of individuals rallying together in solidarity.

Yet, even as we celebrate the progress made and the victories won, we must not lose sight of the daunting challenges that lie ahead. Plastic pollution knows no borders, and its tendrils reach every corner of our planet. The fight against this pervasive menace demands a concerted, sustained, and unwavering commitment from all sectors of society.

In the pages that follow, readers will find not only a call to action but also a roadmap for change. Through education, advocacy, and collective action, we can turn the tide on plastic pollution and safeguard the future of our oceans and the communities that depend on them.

May **Tides of Change** serve as a beacon of hope and a catalyst for transformation in the ongoing struggle to mitigate plastic pollution in Small Island Developing States.

**With Unwavering Resolve,
Dr. Chirag Bhimani**

About the Book

Plastic pollution has emerged as one of the most pressing environmental challenges of our time, with profound implications for ecosystems, economies, and societies worldwide. Nowhere is this more evident than in Small Island Developing States (SIDS), where the convergence of factors such as limited land availability, fragile ecosystems, and heavy reliance on marine resources exacerbates the impacts of plastic pollution. However, amidst these challenges lie opportunities for innovation, collaboration, and sustainable development.

Tides of Change: Mitigating Plastic Pollution in Small Island Developing States seeks to inform, inspire, and empower readers to join the global effort to combat plastic pollution and safeguard the world's oceans for future generations.

Chapter - 1
Introduction

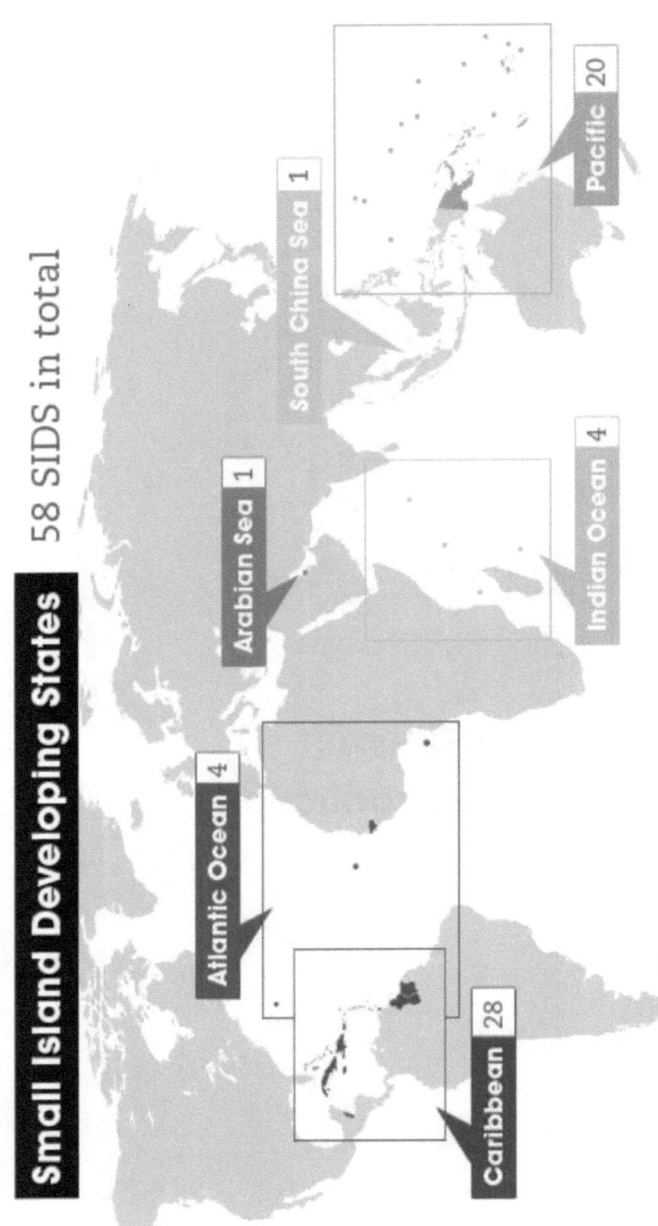

Introduction

This chapter provides an overview of the extent of plastic pollution globally and delves into the specific vulnerabilities of SIDS. It explores the interconnectedness of land-based and marine sources of plastic pollution and examines how plastic waste travels across vast oceanic currents, affecting even the most remote island nations.

Plastic pollution is a global crisis that knows no borders. From the bustling metropolises of the world's largest cities to the remote shores of uninhabited islands, plastic waste has become an omnipresent threat to our planet's ecosystems and human well-being. Nowhere is this threat more acute than in Small Island Developing States (SIDS), where the convergence of geographical, socio-economic, and environmental factors magnifies the impacts of plastic pollution.

Understanding the Scope of Plastic Pollution

Plastic pollution is a multifaceted challenge that encompasses a wide array of sources, pathways, and consequences. Every year, millions of metric tons of plastic waste enter our oceans, rivers, and landfills, posing a grave threat to marine life, coastal communities, and global ecosystems. From plastic bags and bottles to microplastics and abandoned fishing gear, the sheer diversity and ubiquity of plastic waste present a formidable challenge to conservation efforts worldwide.

The scope of plastic pollution extends far beyond the visible litter strewn along beaches and waterways. Microplastics, tiny particles less than five millimetres in size, have infiltrated even the most remote and pristine environments, posing a hidden menace to marine organisms and human health alike. Meanwhile, macroplastics, such as derelict fishing gear and industrial debris, continue to wreak havoc on marine ecosystems, entangling wildlife and disrupting fragile habitats.

Despite growing awareness of the problem, the scale of plastic pollution continues to escalate, driven by unsustainable consumption patterns, inadequate waste management infrastructure, and the proliferation of single-use plastics. Addressing this complex and pervasive challenge requires a concerted effort at the local, national, and international levels, guided by sound science, effective policies, and meaningful action.

The Vulnerability of Small Island Developing States (SIDS)

Small Island Developing States (SIDS) are among the most vulnerable to the impacts of plastic pollution, owing to their unique geographic, economic, and environmental circumstances. Characterized by small landmasses, limited natural resources, and high population densities, SIDS face disproportionate risks from the indiscriminate proliferation of plastic waste.

One of the most immediate threats posed by plastic pollution to SIDS is its impact on marine ecosystems and coastal biodiversity. With economies heavily reliant on fisheries, tourism, and marine resources, SIDS are acutely sensitive to disruptions in marine ecosystems caused by plastic pollution. Coral reefs, mangrove forests, and seagrass meadows, which provide essential habitat and sustenance for countless species, are increasingly imperilled by plastic debris.

Furthermore, the socio-economic ramifications of plastic pollution extend far beyond the ecological realm. Coastal communities in SIDS often bear the brunt of plastic pollution, grappling with contaminated beaches, polluted waterways, and diminished livelihood opportunities. The tourism industry, a linchpin of many SIDS economies, is particularly vulnerable to the reputational damage wrought by plastic pollution, as visitors shun destinations plagued by litter and pollution.

In addition to its environmental and economic toll, plastic pollution also undermines the cultural heritage and identity of SIDS communities. For millennia, island cultures have maintained a deep spiritual and cultural connection to the ocean, viewing it as a source of sustenance, inspiration, and reverence. Today, this sacred bond is threatened by the pervasive presence of plastic waste, which desecrates sacred sites, contaminates traditional fishing grounds, and erodes the cultural fabric of SIDS societies.

In light of these pressing challenges, the need for concerted action to mitigate plastic pollution in Small Island Developing States (SIDS) has never been greater. This book, "Tides of Change: Mitigating Plastic Pollution in Small Island Developing States," seeks to explore the root causes of plastic pollution, showcase innovative solutions, and inspire collective action to safeguard the fragile ecosystems and vibrant communities of SIDS for generations to come.

Chapter - 2
The Impact of Plastic Pollution on SIDS

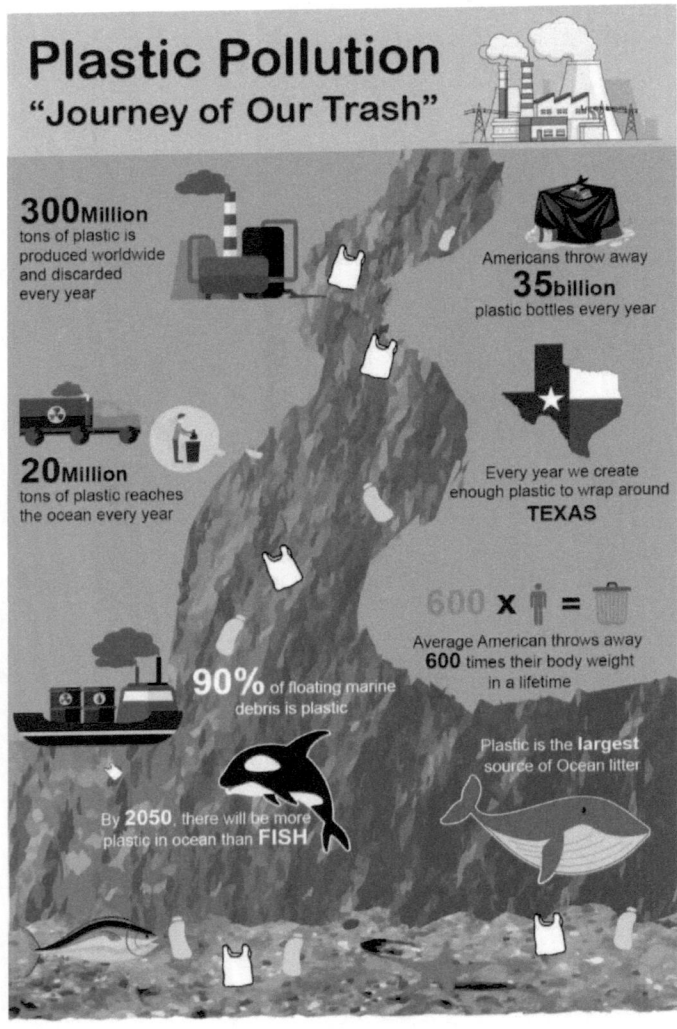

The Impact of Plastic Pollution on SIDS

Plastic pollution exacts a heavy toll on the environment, economy, and social fabric of SIDS. From endangering marine life and coral reefs to undermining tourism and fisheries industries, the consequences are manifold. This chapter examines these impacts in detail, shedding light on the disproportionate burden borne by SIDS communities.

Small Island Developing States (SIDS) are uniquely vulnerable to the impacts of plastic pollution, facing ecological, economic, and social consequences that threaten their very existence. This chapter explores the multifaceted nature of these impacts and the urgent need for action to mitigate them.

Ecological Consequences

Plastic pollution poses a grave threat to the fragile ecosystems of Small Island Developing States (SIDS), which are renowned for their rich biodiversity and pristine natural landscapes. In this chapter, we delve into the ecological consequences of plastic pollution on SIDS, examining how it impacts terrestrial and marine ecosystems, disrupts food webs, and undermines the health and resilience of these island nations.

1. Terrestrial Ecosystems

Plastic pollution does not confine itself to the marine environment; it also infiltrates terrestrial ecosystems, including coastal areas, beaches, and inland habitats. Plastic debris can smother vegetation, alter soil composition, and leach harmful chemicals into the surrounding environment, posing risks to plant and animal life. In SIDS, where land resources are limited and biodiversity is particularly vulnerable, the presence of plastic pollution threatens the integrity of terrestrial ecosystems and compromises their ability to support native flora and fauna.

2. Marine Ecosystems

The marine environment is particularly susceptible to the impacts of plastic pollution, with SIDS bearing a disproportionate burden due to their extensive coastlines and reliance on marine resources. Plastic debris poses a direct threat to marine life through ingestion, entanglement, and habitat destruction. Sea turtles, seabirds, and marine mammals are especially vulnerable, mistaking plastic fragments for food or becoming ensnared in discarded fishing gear. Moreover, microplastics–tiny particles resulting from the breakdown of larger plastic items–accumulate in the marine food chain, with potential implications for ecosystem health and biodiversity.

3. Coral Reefs

Coral reefs are among the most biodiverse and economically valuable ecosystems in SIDS, providing essential habitat for countless species and supporting tourism and fisheries industries. However, plastic pollution jeopardizes the health and resilience of coral reefs, contributing to coral bleaching, disease outbreaks, and impaired reproductive success. Plastic debris can physically damage coral colonies, block sunlight, and introduce toxic substances, exacerbating the stressors already facing these vulnerable ecosystems.

4. Impacts on Fisheries and Aquatic Resources

SIDS rely heavily on fisheries and aquaculture for food security, livelihoods, and cultural identity. However, plastic pollution threatens the sustainability of marine resources, compromising fish stocks, contaminating seafood, and undermining traditional fishing practices. Ghost fishing gear, abandoned or lost at sea, continues to trap marine life indiscriminately, posing a persistent threat to the health of coastal ecosystems and the livelihoods of fishing communities.

5. Ecosystem Services and Resilience

Beyond their intrinsic value, ecosystems in SIDS provide a range of vital services, including coastal protection, carbon sequestration, and cultural heritage. Plastic pollution jeopardizes these ecosystem services, diminishing the resilience of SIDS to environmental hazards such as coastal erosion, storm surges, and climate change impacts. By degrading natural habitats and disrupting ecological processes, plastic pollution undermines the capacity of SIDS to adapt and thrive in the face of ongoing environmental challenges.

Hence, the ecological consequences of plastic pollution on Small Island Developing States are profound and far-reaching, threatening the very foundation of their natural heritage and sustainable development. Addressing this complex issue requires holistic approaches that prioritize ecosystem conservation, waste management, and sustainable livelihoods. Only through concerted action and collective stewardship can we safeguard the ecological integrity of SIDS and ensure a brighter future for generations to come.

Economic Implications

Plastic pollution poses significant economic challenges for Small Island Developing States (SIDS), impacting key sectors such as tourism, fisheries, and agriculture. This chapter explores the intricate relationship between plastic pollution and the economic well-being of SIDS, shedding light on the direct and indirect costs incurred by these vulnerable nations.

1. Tourism

SIDS rely heavily on tourism as a major source of revenue and employment. However, plastic pollution detracts from the natural beauty and pristine environments that attract tourists to these islands. Beaches strewn with plastic debris not only deter visitors but also diminish the overall tourism experience. As a result, SIDS may experience a decline in tourist arrivals, leading to revenue losses and job displacement in the tourism industry.

2. Fisheries

The fishing industry is a vital economic lifeline for many SIDS, providing income, food security, and livelihoods for coastal communities. However, plastic pollution poses serious threats to marine ecosystems and fish populations. Plastic debris can entangle marine animals, damage coral reefs, and contaminate fish stocks. In addition to ecological harm, plastic ingestion by fish can have detrimental effects on human health and food safety. As a consequence, SIDS may face reduced fishery yields, increased health risks, and diminished economic returns from fishing activities.

3. Coastal Infrastructure and Cleanup Costs

Plastic pollution imposes direct costs on SIDS through the need for coastal cleanup efforts and infrastructure maintenance. Local governments and municipalities bear the financial burden of removing plastic waste from beaches, shorelines, and coastal waters. Moreover, the accumulation of plastic debris can exacerbate erosion, degrade infrastructure such as harbours and ports, and impede marine transportation routes. The expenses associated with mitigating these impacts further strain already limited financial resources in SIDS.

4. Brand and Reputation Damage

The prevalence of plastic pollution in SIDS can tarnish their international reputation and brand image. Negative media coverage and public perception of environmental degradation may deter foreign investment, donor support, and international partnerships. Furthermore, SIDS may face pressure from consumers, businesses, and advocacy groups demanding action to address plastic pollution, which could impact trade relations and market access for key exports.

5. Long-term Economic Sustainability

Plastic pollution undermines the long-term economic sustainability of SIDS by eroding natural capital, diminishing ecosystem services, and undermining sustainable development goals. Persistent plastic waste hampers the growth of eco-tourism initiatives, threatens the viability of traditional livelihoods reliant on healthy marine ecosystems, and increases the vulnerability of SIDS to external economic shocks and environmental disasters.

6. Opportunities for Economic Resilience

Despite the economic challenges posed by plastic pollution, there are opportunities for SIDS to build economic resilience and foster sustainable growth. Investing in waste management infrastructure, promoting eco-friendly tourism practices, and supporting sustainable fisheries management can help mitigate the economic impacts of plastic pollution while creating new opportunities for innovation, entrepreneurship, and green economic development.

Thus, the economic implications of plastic pollution on SIDS are profound and multifaceted, encompassing both direct and indirect costs across key sectors of the economy. Addressing plastic pollution requires concerted action at the local, national, and international levels to safeguard the economic prosperity and resilience of SIDS for future generations.

Social and Cultural Effects

Plastic pollution exacts a heavy toll on the social and cultural fabric of Small Island Developing States (SIDS), intertwining with the daily lives, traditions, and identities of their inhabitants. In this chapter, we explore the profound social and cultural effects of plastic pollution in SIDS, shedding light on the ways in which it shapes communities and challenges their resilience.

Social Disruption and Health Concerns

Plastic pollution disrupts social cohesion and community well-being in SIDS in various ways. As plastic waste accumulates on beaches, in coastal areas, and in marine ecosystems, it degrades the natural beauty that is often central to local identities and economies. This degradation can undermine tourism, a vital source of income for many SIDS, and erode the sense of pride and connection that communities feel towards their environment.

Moreover, plastic pollution poses significant health risks to SIDS populations. Plastic debris can entangle marine life, contaminate food sources, and leach harmful chemicals into the environment, threatening both human and animal health. Inadequate waste management systems exacerbate these risks, leading to pollution of freshwater sources and exposure to toxic substances.

Cultural Heritage and Identity

For many SIDS, the ocean is not only a source of livelihood but also a central aspect of cultural identity and heritage. Traditional practices such as fishing, seafaring, and ocean-based ceremonies are deeply intertwined with local cultures and belief systems. However, plastic pollution undermines these cultural traditions by desecrating sacred sites, disrupting marine ecosystems, and diminishing the abundance of marine resources.

Plastic pollution also challenges the sustainability of cultural practices that rely on natural materials and resources. For example, traditional handicrafts made from materials such as palm fronds, coconut husks, and seashells are increasingly replaced by plastic-based alternatives due to the pervasiveness of plastic waste. This shift not only threatens the authenticity of cultural expressions but also contributes to the cycle of plastic pollution.

Community Resilience and Adaptive Strategies

Despite these challenges, SIDS communities demonstrate remarkable resilience and innovation in the face of plastic pollution. Community-led clean-up efforts, recycling initiatives, and awareness-raising campaigns are increasingly common across SIDS, reflecting a growing recognition of the importance of addressing plastic pollution at the grassroots level.

Moreover, many SIDS draw on their rich cultural heritage and traditional knowledge systems to develop adaptive strategies for coping with plastic pollution. For example, some communities incorporate indigenous practices of resource management and conservation into modern waste management systems, emphasizing the interconnectedness of human and environmental health.

Empowerment and Advocacy

As awareness of the social and cultural effects of plastic pollution grows, SIDS communities are becoming increasingly vocal and engaged in advocacy efforts to address the issue. Local activists, youth groups, and community organizations play a pivotal role in raising awareness, mobilizing resources, and holding governments and corporations accountable for their contributions to plastic pollution.

Furthermore, SIDS are leveraging their collective voice on the global stage to advocate for stronger action on plastic pollution. Through regional alliances, international partnerships, and participation in multilateral forums, SIDS are amplifying their concerns and calling for concerted efforts to combat plastic pollution and protect the oceans that sustain their way of life.

The social and cultural effects of plastic pollution in SIDS are profound and multifaceted, touching every aspect of community life and challenging the resilience of these vulnerable island nations. By recognizing the interconnectedness of social, cultural, and environmental issues, we can develop more holistic approaches to mitigating plastic pollution in SIDS and building sustainable futures for their inhabitants.

In summary, plastic pollution exacts a heavy toll on the ecological, economic, and social well-being of Small Island Developing States. Urgent action is needed to mitigate these impacts and protect the fragile ecosystems and livelihoods of these vulnerable island nations. Through concerted efforts at the local, national, and international levels, we can strive to build a more sustainable and resilient future for SIDS and safeguard the world's oceans for generations to come

Chapter - 3
Root Causes of Plastic Pollution

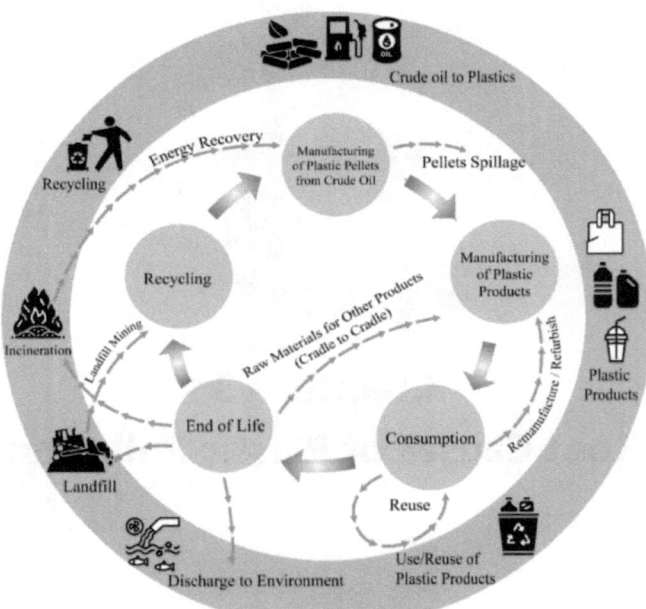

Root Causes of Plastic Pollution

To effectively address plastic pollution, it is essential to understand its underlying causes. This chapter analyses the role of consumer behaviour, inadequate waste management infrastructure, and the pervasive influence of single-use plastics and packaging in perpetuating the problem.

Plastic pollution in Small Island Developing States (SIDS) is a multifaceted issue with deep-rooted causes that demand comprehensive solutions. Understanding these root causes is essential for devising effective strategies to mitigate plastic pollution and foster sustainable development in SIDS. This chapter explores three primary contributors to plastic pollution: consumer behaviour, inadequate waste management systems, and the proliferation of single-use plastics and packaging.

Consumer Behaviour

Consumer behaviour plays a central role in driving the demand for and proliferation of single-use plastics in Small Island Developing States (SIDS). From the choices individuals make at the point of purchase to their disposal habits, these actions collectively contribute to the accumulation of plastic waste in the environment. In this chapter, we delve into the various aspects of consumer behaviour that serve as root causes of plastic pollution in SIDS, exploring underlying motivations, cultural influences, and opportunities for behavioural change.

Understanding Consumer Behaviour

Consumer behaviour encompasses the actions, decisions, and motivations of individuals or households when acquiring, using, and disposing of goods and services. In the context of plastic pollution, understanding why consumers choose certain products, how they use them, and what factors influence their disposal habits is crucial for designing effective interventions.

Factors Driving Plastic Consumption

Several factors drive the widespread consumption of single-use plastics in SIDS:

1. **Convenience:** Single-use plastics are often favoured for their convenience, particularly in fast-paced lifestyles where time is of the essence. Items like plastic bags, bottles, and packaging offer quick and easy solutions for on-the-go consumption.

2. **Cost:** In some cases, single-use plastics are perceived as more affordable alternatives to reusable or sustainable options. This perception of cost-effectiveness can influence consumer choices, especially in regions where disposable income is limited.

3. **Marketing and Advertising:** The power of marketing and advertising cannot be underestimated in shaping consumer preferences. The promotion of plastic products through persuasive messaging, branding, and packaging design can influence consumer behaviour and drive demand.

4. **Lack of Alternatives:** In many SIDS, limited access to alternatives to single-use plastics exacerbates reliance on these materials. The availability of sustainable alternatives such as reusable bags, containers, and biodegradable packaging may be limited or prohibitively expensive.

Cultural Influences

Cultural norms, traditions, and social practices also play a significant role in shaping consumer behaviour and attitudes towards plastic use. In some SIDS, there may be cultural practices that contribute to plastic pollution, such as the use of plastic-based materials in ceremonies, festivals, or everyday rituals. Additionally, societal attitudes towards waste management and environmental conservation can vary, influencing individual behaviours regarding plastic disposal and recycling.

Opportunities for Behavioural Change

While consumer behaviour is deeply entrenched and influenced by various factors, there are opportunities for meaningful change:

1. Education and Awareness:

Increasing public awareness about the environmental impacts of plastic pollution is essential for fostering behaviour change. Educational campaigns, school programs, and community outreach initiatives can empower individuals to make more sustainable choices.

2. Incentives and Disincentives:

Government policies and incentives can help incentivize sustainable behaviour and discourage plastic consumption. This may include measures such as plastic bag bans, taxes on single-use plastics, or deposit-return schemes for plastic bottles.

3. Product Innovation:

The development of innovative products and packaging alternatives can provide consumers with viable alternatives to single-use plastics. From biodegradable materials to reusable packaging solutions, innovation in product design can help shift consumer preferences towards more sustainable options.

4. Community Engagement:

Engaging local communities in waste management and recycling initiatives can foster a sense of collective responsibility and ownership over environmental issues. Community clean-up events, recycling drives, and waste reduction campaigns can mobilize individuals to take action against plastic pollution.

Thus, consumer behaviour is a significant driver of plastic pollution in Small Island Developing States, but it also presents an opportunity for meaningful change. By understanding the factors that influence consumer choices, addressing cultural influences, and promoting alternatives, we can work towards creating a more sustainable future where plastic pollution is mitigated, and the health of our oceans and islands is preserved for generations to come.

Inadequate Waste Management Systems

Plastic pollution in Small Island Developing States (SIDS) is often exacerbated by inadequate waste management systems, which struggle to cope with the increasing volume of plastic waste generated by growing populations and tourism industries. This chapter examines the systemic challenges facing waste management in SIDS, explores the consequences of ineffective waste disposal practices, and identifies opportunities for improvement.

Understanding the Challenge

Small Island Developing States face unique geographical and infrastructural challenges that complicate waste management efforts. Limited land availability, dispersed populations, and susceptibility to natural disasters such as hurricanes and tsunamis pose significant obstacles to establishing robust waste management infrastructure. Additionally, many SIDS rely heavily on tourism, resulting in seasonal spikes in waste generation that strain existing systems.

Consequences of Inadequate Waste Management

1. Land and Marine Pollution:

Insufficient waste disposal facilities lead to open dumping and burning of waste, contaminating land and marine ecosystems. Plastic waste that is not properly managed can end up in rivers and oceans, posing a threat to marine life and coral reefs.

2. Public Health Risks:

Open dumping of waste attracts vermin and pests, creating breeding grounds for disease vectors. Improper disposal of plastic waste can also release harmful chemicals into the environment, posing risks to human health through air and water contamination.

3. Tourism Impact:

SIDS heavily reliant on tourism may suffer reputational damage if inadequate waste management leads to visible pollution of beaches and coastal areas. This can deter tourists and impact the local economy.

4. Climate Change Contribution:

Improper waste management practices, such as open burning of waste, contribute to greenhouse gas emissions, exacerbating climate change impacts on SIDS.

Barriers to Effective Waste Management

Several factors contribute to the inadequacy of waste management systems in SIDS:

1. Limited Resources:

SIDS often lack the financial resources and technical expertise needed to invest in modern waste management infrastructure and technologies.

2. Lack of Awareness and Education:

Public awareness about the importance of proper waste management and the impacts of plastic pollution may be low, leading to apathy and inadequate participation in waste reduction and recycling efforts.

3. Institutional Weaknesses:

Weak governance structures, fragmented institutional responsibilities, and bureaucratic inefficiencies can impede the development and implementation of effective waste management policies and programs.

4. Dependency on Imports:

SIDS often import large quantities of packaged goods, leading to an influx of non-recyclable plastic packaging that overwhelms local waste management systems.

Opportunities for Improvement

1. Integrated Waste Management Systems:

SIDS can benefit from adopting integrated waste management approaches that combine waste reduction, recycling, composting, and energy recovery to minimize the amount of waste sent to landfills or open dumps.

2. Community Engagement and Education:

Increasing public awareness about the importance of waste reduction and recycling through education campaigns, community clean-up events, and school programs can foster a culture of environmental stewardship.

3. Investment in Infrastructure:

Donor support, public-private partnerships, and innovative financing mechanisms can help SIDS invest in modern waste management infrastructure, such as waste-to-energy facilities, recycling centres, and composting facilities.

4. Policy and Regulatory Reforms:

Strengthening waste management policies, regulations, and enforcement mechanisms can help SIDS improve waste collection, segregation, and disposal practices, as well as incentivize the use of sustainable packaging and alternatives to single-use plastics.

Case Study: The Maldives

The Maldives, a SIDS heavily reliant on tourism, has implemented innovative waste management initiatives to address the challenges of plastic pollution. The introduction of decentralized waste management systems, community-based recycling programs, and the establishment of marine protected areas has helped the Maldives mitigate the impacts of plastic pollution on its pristine beaches and marine ecosystems.

Hence, it can be seen that, inadequate waste management systems pose significant challenges to Small Island Developing States in their efforts to combat plastic pollution. Addressing these challenges requires a multi-pronged approach that involves investment in infrastructure, community engagement, policy reforms, and international collaboration. By taking decisive action to strengthen waste management systems, SIDS can reduce their vulnerability to plastic pollution and build more sustainable and resilient communities for the future.

Single-Use Plastics and Packaging

Single-use plastics and packaging represent a significant driver of plastic pollution in Small Island Developing States (SIDS), exacerbating environmental degradation, economic strain, and social challenges. This chapter delves into the root causes of plastic pollution stemming from the pervasive use of single-use plastics and packaging in SIDS, examining their impacts and exploring strategies for mitigation.

The Proliferation of Single-Use Plastics

Single-use plastics, including items such as plastic bags, bottles, straws, utensils, and packaging, have become ubiquitous in modern society. Their convenience and affordability have led to widespread adoption, but this convenience comes at a steep cost. In SIDS, where waste management infrastructure may be limited and recycling facilities scarce, single-use plastics pose a particularly acute problem.

Environmental Impacts

The environmental consequences of single-use plastics in SIDS are profound. Plastic waste litters coastlines, clogs waterways, and accumulates in marine ecosystems, posing a grave threat to marine life. Sea turtles, seabirds, and marine mammals are especially vulnerable to entanglement and ingestion of plastic debris, leading to injury, suffocation, and death. Moreover, plastic pollution undermines the health of coral reefs and marine habitats, disrupting delicate ecosystems and jeopardizing biodiversity.

Economic Strain

The economic impacts of single-use plastics in SIDS are multifaceted. Tourism, a vital source of revenue for many island nations, can suffer from the unsightly presence of plastic litter on beaches and in marine environments, tarnishing the natural beauty that attracts visitors. Additionally, the costs associated with plastic waste management, including collection, transport, and disposal, strain already limited financial resources, diverting funds that could be allocated to critical social services and infrastructure development.

Social Challenges

Plastic pollution exacts a toll on the social fabric of SIDS, affecting public health, cultural practices, and community well-being. Improperly managed plastic waste can contaminate freshwater sources, leading to waterborne diseases and compromising access to safe drinking water. Furthermore, plastic pollution can erode traditional practices and cultural values tied to the land and sea, disrupting intergenerational knowledge transmission and diminishing community cohesion.

Strategies for Mitigation

Addressing the root causes of plastic pollution from single-use plastics and packaging in SIDS requires a multifaceted approach that combines regulatory measures, public awareness campaigns, and industry collaboration.

1. Regulatory Measures:

Governments in SIDS can implement policies to restrict or ban the production, importation, and sale of certain single-use plastics, prioritizing alternatives that are reusable, recyclable, or compostable. Additionally, extended producer responsibility (EPR) schemes can incentivize manufacturers to design products with end-of-life considerations in mind, encouraging innovation and eco-friendly packaging solutions.

2. Public Awareness Campaigns:

Education and outreach initiatives play a crucial role in shifting consumer behaviour and promoting sustainable alternatives to single-use plastics. Public awareness campaigns can raise consciousness about the environmental impacts of plastic pollution, empower individuals to make informed choices, and foster a culture of waste reduction and recycling within communities.

3. Industry Collaboration:

Collaboration between government agencies, businesses, and civil society organizations is essential for implementing effective solutions to plastic pollution. Industry stakeholders can work together to develop innovative packaging designs, invest in recycling infrastructure, and support initiatives that promote circular economy principles, such as product stewardship and resource recovery.

4. Community Engagement:

Engaging local communities in plastic pollution mitigation efforts is key to fostering ownership and sustainability. Community-based initiatives, such as beach cleanups, recycling drives, and plastic-free advocacy groups, empower individuals to take action at the grassroots level, building resilience and fostering social cohesion.

By addressing the root causes of plastic pollution stemming from single-use plastics and packaging in SIDS through a combination of regulatory measures, public awareness campaigns, industry collaboration, and community engagement, we can chart a course towards a more sustainable and resilient future for these vulnerable island nations.

In confronting the root causes of plastic pollution, it is imperative to adopt a holistic approach that addresses consumer behaviour, improves waste management systems, and reduces reliance on single-use plastics. By fostering a culture of sustainability, investing in infrastructure, and promoting innovation, SIDS can chart a course towards a future where plastic pollution is no longer a threat to their ecosystems, economies, and communities.

Dr. Chirag Bhimani

Chapter - 4
Policy and Legislative Frameworks

Sources for plastics

- Extraction / Production / Sale / Consumption
- Transportation
- Lack of waste collection
- Illegal dumping
- Littering
- Careless behaviour

- Low level of recyclability:
  - Plastic composites
  - Multilayered plastics
  - Contaminated plastics
  - Small pieces and fractions of plastics

- Mismanaged at:
  - Collection
  - Transportation
  - Separation
  - Recycling

Fugitive plastics
- Macroplastics
- Microplastics
- Nanoplastics

→ **Systemic impacts**
- Air
- Water
- Soil quality

→ **Cumulative impacts**
- Food chains
- Biodiversity loss
- Climate change

→ **Environmental health impacts**
- Animals
- Plants
- Humans

Policy and Legislative Frameworks

International agreements, national strategies, and regional collaborations play a crucial role in shaping efforts to mitigate plastic pollution in SIDS. This chapter explores the existing policy landscape and identifies opportunities for strengthening regulatory frameworks and enforcement mechanisms.

Plastic pollution knows no borders, and addressing this global challenge requires a multifaceted approach encompassing international cooperation, national strategies, and regional collaboration efforts. In this chapter, we explore the key policy and legislative frameworks that are instrumental in mitigating plastic pollution in Small Island Developing States (SIDS).

International Agreements and Protocols

Small Island Developing States (SIDS) face unique challenges in combating plastic pollution, requiring both national and international cooperation. This chapter explores the role of international agreements and protocols in shaping policy and legislative frameworks aimed at mitigating plastic pollution in SIDS.

1. The Basel Convention on the Control of Transboundary Movements of Hazardous Wastes and Their Disposal

The Basel Convention, adopted in 1989 and entered into force in 1992, aims to regulate the movement of hazardous wastes across borders and minimize their generation. While initially focused on hazardous chemicals and wastes, its scope has been expanded to include plastic waste, particularly in response to the growing global concern over marine plastic pollution. SIDS, as vulnerable coastal nations, benefit from the provisions of the Basel Convention that regulate the transboundary movement of plastic waste and promote environmentally sound management practices.

2. The Stockholm Convention on Persistent Organic Pollutants (POPs)

Persistent organic pollutants (POPs), including certain types of plastic additives and contaminants, pose significant risks to human health and the environment. The Stockholm Convention, established in 2001 and ratified by numerous countries, aims to eliminate or restrict the production, use, and release of POPs. SIDS rely on the Stockholm Convention to address the sources of POPs that contribute to plastic pollution in their marine and terrestrial ecosystems.

3. The United Nations Convention on the Law of the Sea (UNCLOS)

UNCLOS, adopted in 1982 and often referred to as the "constitution for the oceans," provides a comprehensive legal framework for the governance of the world's oceans and seas. SIDS leverage

UNCLOS to assert their rights and responsibilities in managing and conserving marine resources, including addressing plastic pollution within their territorial waters and exclusive economic zones.

4. The Rotterdam Convention on the Prior Informed Consent (PIC) Procedure for Certain Hazardous Chemicals and Pesticides in International Trade

The Rotterdam Convention, established in 1998, aims to promote shared responsibility and cooperation in the international trade of hazardous chemicals and pesticides. While primarily focused on industrial chemicals and agricultural pesticides, its principles of informed consent and information exchange are relevant to the trade and management of plastic products containing hazardous substances. SIDS utilize the Rotterdam Convention to enhance transparency and control over the importation of potentially harmful plastics.

5. The Regional Seas Conventions and Action Plans

Several Regional Seas Conventions and Action Plans exist around the world, including the Caribbean Environment Programme (Cartagena Convention), the Pacific Islands Regional Programme (SPREP), and the Nairobi Convention for the Western Indian Ocean. These regional agreements facilitate collaboration among neighbouring countries to address shared environmental challenges, including plastic pollution. SIDS participate in these conventions to develop coordinated approaches to marine litter prevention, cleanup, and sustainable waste management.

6. The Paris Agreement under the United Nations Framework Convention on Climate Change (UNFCCC)

While not specifically focused on plastic pollution, the Paris Agreement represents a landmark international commitment to combat climate change and its impacts, which are intricately linked to marine ecosystems and plastic pollution. SIDS advocate for ambitious climate action under the Paris Agreement to mitigate the drivers of plastic pollution, such as carbon emissions and sea level rise, while also promoting resilience-building measures.

Thus, International agreements and protocols play a crucial role in providing a framework for cooperation and action on plastic pollution in Small Island Developing States. By leveraging these agreements, SIDS can strengthen their policy and legislative frameworks, enhance their capacity for environmental management, and work collaboratively towards a cleaner and healthier marine environment.

National Strategies and Initiatives

In the battle against plastic pollution, the formulation and implementation of robust national strategies and initiatives are critical for Small Island

Developing States (SIDS). This chapter examines the various approaches adopted by SIDS governments to address plastic pollution through policy and legislative frameworks, highlighting both successes and challenges.

1. Policy Development Process

➤ Stakeholder Engagement:

SIDS governments often engage stakeholders from diverse sectors, including government agencies, non-governmental organizations (NGOs), businesses, academia, and local communities, in the policy development process. This inclusive approach helps ensure that policies are comprehensive, relevant, and reflective of the needs and perspectives of all stakeholders.

➤ Scientific Research and Data Analysis:

Evidence-based policymaking is essential for effectively addressing plastic pollution. SIDS governments invest in scientific research and data collection efforts to better understand the sources, pathways, and impacts of plastic pollution in their respective territories. This scientific evidence informs policy decisions and enables governments to prioritize interventions where they are most needed.

➢ Adaptation and Innovation:

SIDS face unique challenges in combating plastic pollution due to their geographical, ecological, and socio-economic characteristics. National strategies and initiatives must be tailored to the specific circumstances of each SIDS, taking into account factors such as population density, waste generation rates, infrastructure limitations, and cultural practices. Innovative approaches, such as community-based recycling programs and eco-friendly packaging incentives, are increasingly being explored to address these challenges.

2. Legislative Frameworks

➤ Regulatory Measures:

SIDS governments enact laws and regulations to regulate the production, use, and disposal of plastics within their jurisdictions. These regulatory measures may include bans or restrictions on single-use plastics, extended producer responsibility (EPR) schemes, deposit-refund systems, and incentives for the use of biodegradable and compostable materials. By establishing clear rules and standards, governments create a conducive environment for sustainable practices and encourage compliance among businesses and consumers.

➤ Enforcement Mechanisms:

Effective enforcement of plastic pollution regulations is essential to ensure compliance and deter illicit activities. SIDS governments invest in enforcement mechanisms such as monitoring and surveillance programs, inspection regimes, penalties for non-compliance, and public awareness campaigns to educate the populace about their responsibilities and the consequences of plastic pollution. Collaborative efforts between government agencies, law enforcement bodies, and civil society organizations strengthen enforcement efforts and promote accountability.

➤ International Cooperation:

Plastic pollution knows no boundaries, and SIDS recognize the importance of international cooperation in addressing this global challenge. SIDS governments participate in regional and international forums, such as the United Nations Environment Assembly (UNEA) and the Convention on Biological Diversity (CBD), to exchange knowledge, share best practices, and coordinate joint actions to combat plastic pollution. By leveraging collective resources and expertise, SIDS amplify their impact and contribute to global efforts to protect marine environments and biodiversity.

3. Capacity Building and Technical Assistance

➤ Training and Education:

Building the capacity of government officials, waste management professionals, and community leaders is essential for the effective implementation of plastic pollution mitigation measures. SIDS governments invest in training programs, workshops, and educational campaigns to enhance awareness, knowledge, and skills related to waste management, recycling technologies, pollution prevention, and sustainable consumption and production practices.

➤ Technical Assistance and Funding Support:

Many SIDS face resource constraints in their efforts to combat plastic pollution. International organizations, development partners, and donor agencies provide technical assistance, capacity-building support, and financial resources to help SIDS develop and implement national strategies and initiatives. Grants, loans, and technical expertise facilitate the establishment of waste management infrastructure, the adoption of innovative technologies, and the implementation of community-based projects aimed at reducing plastic pollution.

4. Monitoring and Evaluation

➤ Performance Metrics:

SIDS governments establish monitoring and evaluation frameworks to track progress towards plastic pollution mitigation goals and objectives. Key performance indicators may include reduction targets for plastic waste generation, improvements in waste management infrastructure, increases in recycling rates, and reductions in marine litter. Regular reporting and data analysis enable governments to assess the effectiveness of policy interventions, identify areas for improvement, and adjust strategies as needed.

> **Transparency and Accountability:**

Transparency and accountability are essential principles in the governance of plastic pollution mitigation efforts. SIDS governments publish reports, conduct audits, and engage with stakeholders to provide updates on progress, share lessons learned, and solicit feedback on policy implementation. By fostering a culture of transparency and accountability, governments enhance public trust and confidence in their actions and promote active participation in plastic pollution mitigation initiatives.

5. Success Stories and Lessons Learned

> **Case Studies:**

Throughout the world, SIDS have implemented a range of successful strategies and initiatives to mitigate plastic pollution. Case studies from countries such as Seychelles, Maldives, Barbados, and Fiji demonstrate innovative approaches to waste management, community engagement, policy development, and international cooperation. These success stories offer valuable lessons and insights for other SIDS facing similar challenges.

➢ Challenges and Opportunities:

Despite progress made, SIDS continue to face numerous challenges in their efforts to combat plastic pollution. These challenges include limited financial resources, inadequate waste management infrastructure, capacity constraints, and competing development priorities. However, these challenges also present opportunities for innovation, collaboration, and sustainable development. By addressing the root causes of plastic pollution and building resilience in coastal communities, SIDS can unlock new pathways to prosperity and environmental stewardship.

In conclusion, national strategies and initiatives play a pivotal role in the policy and legislative frameworks for mitigating plastic pollution in Small Island Developing States. By adopting a holistic approach that integrates scientific evidence, regulatory measures, capacity-building efforts, and international cooperation, SIDS governments can effectively address the complex challenges posed by plastic pollution and pave the way for a more sustainable and resilient future.

Regional Collaboration Efforts

Small Island Developing States (SIDS) face unique challenges in addressing plastic pollution due to their limited resources, geographical isolation, and shared ecosystems. Recognizing the transboundary nature of marine pollution, SIDS have increasingly turned to regional collaboration as a cornerstone of their policy and legislative frameworks. This chapter explores the importance of regional cooperation in mitigating plastic pollution and highlights key initiatives and partnerships aimed at enhancing the resilience of SIDS communities.

Understanding Regional Collaboration

Regional collaboration involves SIDS working together within their respective geographic regions to address common challenges and achieve shared goals. In the context of plastic pollution, regional collaboration enables SIDS to pool resources, share best practices, and coordinate efforts to mitigate the impacts of plastic waste on marine environments and coastal communities.

Regional Organizations and Platforms

Several regional organizations and platforms have been established to facilitate collaboration among SIDS in addressing environmental issues, including plastic pollution. These organizations provide a forum for SIDS to exchange knowledge, coordinate initiatives, and advocate for collective action on regional and international stages. Examples include:

1. Pacific Islands Forum (PIF):

The PIF is a regional intergovernmental organization that brings together 18 SIDS in the

Pacific region. Through its Sustainable Development Programme and Environmental Sustainability Strategy, the PIF promotes regional cooperation on environmental issues, including marine pollution and plastic waste management.

2. Caribbean Community (CARICOM):

CARICOM is a regional integration organization comprising 15 member states and 5 associate members in the Caribbean region. CARICOM's Environment Programme focuses on addressing environmental challenges, including marine pollution and climate change, through regional collaboration and policy coordination.

3. Indian Ocean Rim Association (IORA):

IORA is a regional forum that promotes cooperation and economic integration among Indian Ocean rim countries, including several SIDS. IORA's Working Group on Maritime Safety and Security addresses issues such as marine pollution and environmental protection in the Indian Ocean region.

Policy Harmonization and Standardization

One of the key objectives of regional collaboration is to harmonize policies and regulations across SIDS, ensuring consistency and coherence in approaches to plastic pollution mitigation. By harmonizing policies, SIDS can create a conducive regulatory environment for implementing effective waste management strategies, promoting sustainable practices, and enforcing compliance with international agreements and conventions.

Joint Initiatives and Action Plans

Regional collaboration enables SIDS to develop joint initiatives and action plans to address plastic pollution collectively. These initiatives may include regional waste management programs, capacity-building workshops, research partnerships, and public awareness campaigns. By pooling resources and expertise, SIDS can leverage economies of scale and achieve greater impact in tackling plastic pollution at the regional level.

Cross-Border Cooperation and Information Sharing

Plastic pollution knows no borders, and regional collaboration facilitates cross-border cooperation and information sharing among SIDS. By exchanging data, experiences, and lessons learned, SIDS can enhance their understanding of plastic pollution trends, identify emerging threats, and develop targeted interventions to address shared challenges. Cross-border cooperation also fosters networking and partnerships among government agencies, research institutions, civil society organizations, and the private sector.

Challenges and Opportunities

While regional collaboration offers significant opportunities for SIDS in mitigating plastic pollution, it also presents challenges that must be addressed. These challenges may include differences in policy priorities, resource constraints, institutional capacity gaps, and competing interests among member states. However, by overcoming these challenges through dialogue, consensus-building, and mutual support, SIDS can harness the collective strength of regional collaboration to create a more sustainable future for their communities and the planet.

Regional collaboration is essential for SIDS in developing effective policy and legislative frameworks to mitigate plastic pollution. By working together, SIDS can leverage their collective strengths, resources, and expertise to address common challenges, promote sustainable development, and safeguard the marine environment for future generations. Through ongoing collaboration and cooperation, SIDS can pave the way for a cleaner, healthier, and more resilient future for all.

Conclusion

Policy and legislative frameworks are essential pillars in the fight against plastic pollution in Small Island Developing States. By aligning international agreements with national strategies and fostering regional collaboration efforts, SIDS can strengthen their capacity to address this pressing environmental challenge effectively. However, the success of these efforts ultimately depends on the commitment and cooperation of governments, civil society, the private sector, and the international community as a whole.

In the next chapter, we will delve into innovative solutions that hold promise in mitigating plastic pollution in SIDS, ranging from waste reduction and recycling programs to the adoption of sustainable alternatives to plastic.

Chapter - 5
Innovative Solutions

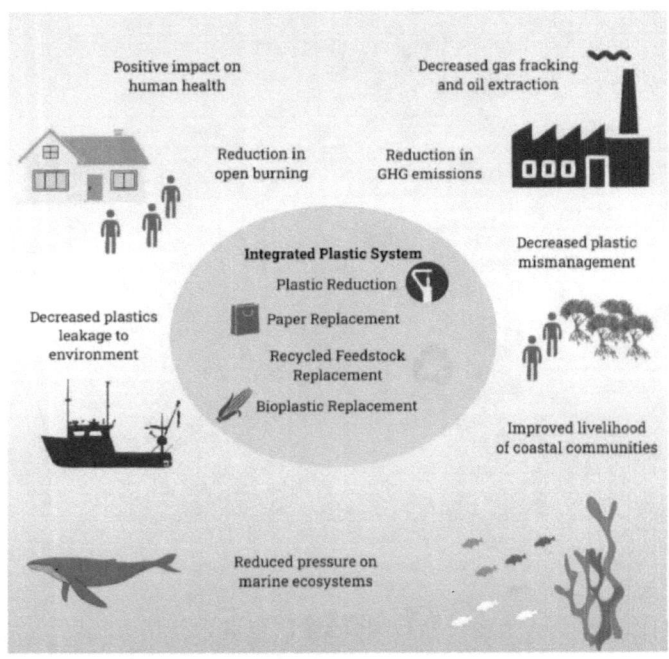

Innovative Solutions

In the face of daunting challenges, SIDS are pioneering innovative solutions to combat plastic pollution. This chapter showcases a range of initiatives, from waste reduction and recycling programs to the adoption of sustainable alternatives to plastic.

Inspite of mounting plastic pollution challenges, Small Island Developing States (SIDS) are pioneering innovative solutions to mitigate the impact on their fragile ecosystems and communities. This chapter explores three key pillars of innovation: Waste Reduction and Recycling Programs, Sustainable Alternatives to Plastic, and Community Engagement and Education.

Waste Reduction and Recycling Programs

Small Island Developing States (SIDS) face unique challenges in managing their waste, particularly plastic waste, due to limited land availability, fragile ecosystems, and vulnerability to climate change impacts. However, innovative solutions tailored to the specific needs and circumstances of SIDS are emerging to address these challenges. This chapter explores a range of innovative waste reduction and recycling programs that offer promising avenues for mitigating plastic pollution in SIDS.

1. Community-Led Recycling Initiatives

Community-led recycling initiatives empower local residents to take ownership of waste management processes. These initiatives often involve the establishment of community recycling centres or collection points where residents can deposit recyclable materials such as plastics, glass, and paper. In SIDS, community-led programs promote environmental stewardship, foster a sense of collective responsibility, and contribute to the circular economy by diverting recyclable materials from landfills and incinerators.

2. Deposit Return Schemes

Deposit return schemes incentivize consumers to return beverage containers for recycling by offering a refundable deposit upon return. In SIDS, where beverage container litter is a common sight, deposit return schemes can significantly reduce plastic pollution by encouraging consumers to properly dispose of their empty bottles and cans. These schemes promote a culture of reuse and recycling while providing economic opportunities for waste collectors and recyclers.

3. Plastic Bottle Recycling Initiatives

Plastic bottle recycling initiatives focus on increasing the collection and recycling of PET (polyethylene terephthalate) bottles, which are commonly used for beverages and personal care products. In SIDS, where bottled water consumption is often high due to concerns about water quality, plastic bottle recycling initiatives play a crucial role in diverting PET bottles from landfills and marine environments. These initiatives may involve partnerships with beverage companies, waste management firms, and local governments to establish collection infrastructure and recycling facilities.

4. Upcycling and Creative Reuse Programs

Upcycling and creative reuse programs transform discarded materials into new and valuable products, thereby extending their lifespan and reducing the demand for virgin materials. In SIDS, where natural resources may be scarce and imported goods are expensive, upcycling initiatives offer sustainable alternatives to conventional consumption patterns. These programs may involve collaborations with local artisans, designers, and entrepreneurs to create innovative products from recycled materials, such as jewellery, fashion accessories, and home decor items.

5. Mobile Recycling Units and Outreach Campaigns

Mobile recycling units and outreach campaigns bring waste reduction and recycling services directly to communities, particularly those in remote or underserved areas. In SIDS, where access to formal waste management infrastructure may be limited, mobile recycling units provide a flexible and adaptable solution for engaging residents and raising awareness about the importance of waste separation and recycling. These initiatives may incorporate educational workshops, demonstrations, and community events to promote behaviour change and foster environmental consciousness.

6. Waste-to-Energy Technologies

Waste-to-energy technologies convert non-recyclable waste materials into energy through processes such as incineration, pyrolysis, and anaerobic digestion. In SIDS, where land availability for landfilling is limited and energy demand is high, waste-to-energy technologies offer a sustainable solution for managing residual waste streams while generating renewable energy. These technologies may be integrated into existing waste management infrastructure or deployed as standalone facilities to reduce dependence on fossil fuels and mitigate greenhouse gas emissions.

7. Partnerships with the Private Sector

Partnerships with the private sector play a critical role in driving innovation and investment in waste reduction and recycling programs in SIDS. Beverage companies, packaging manufacturers, and retailers can collaborate with governments, NGOs, and community organizations to implement extended producer responsibility (EPR) schemes, develop sustainable packaging solutions, and support recycling infrastructure development. These partnerships leverage the resources, expertise, and market influence of the private sector to accelerate progress towards a circular economy and reduce plastic pollution in SIDS.

Innovative solutions for waste reduction and recycling programs in Small Island Developing States offer hope for a more sustainable future where plastic pollution is minimized, natural resources are conserved, and communities thrive in harmony with their environment. By embracing creativity, collaboration, and commitment, SIDS can lead the way towards a circular economy where waste is viewed as a valuable resource rather than a disposable burden.

Sustainable Alternatives to Plastic

Transitioning away from single-use plastics toward sustainable alternatives is a key strategy for reducing plastic pollution in SIDS. From biodegradable packaging to innovative materials made from renewable resources, a wide range of alternatives are emerging to meet the diverse needs of island communities.

Plastic pollution poses a significant threat to the fragile ecosystems and economies of Small Island Developing States (SIDS). To combat this challenge, innovative solutions are essential. This chapter explores a range of sustainable alternatives to plastic and innovative initiatives being implemented in SIDS to reduce plastic consumption, promote recycling, and foster a culture of environmental stewardship.

1. Biodegradable and Compostable Alternatives

One promising avenue for reducing plastic pollution in SIDS is the adoption of biodegradable and compostable alternatives to traditional plastic products. These materials, derived from renewable resources such as plant-based polymers or bioplastics, offer similar functionality to conventional plastics but degrade more quickly and harmlessly in the environment. In SIDS, initiatives to promote biodegradable packaging for food and beverages, compostable cutlery and utensils, and bioplastic shopping bags are gaining traction, offering consumers eco-friendly alternatives without compromising convenience.

2. Natural Fibre Products

SIDS are rich in natural resources, including abundant plant fibres that can be utilized as alternatives to plastic. Coconut husks, banana leaves, and bamboo are just a few examples of readily available materials that can be transformed into biodegradable and sustainable products such as packaging, containers, and utensils. By harnessing these local resources, SIDS can reduce their reliance on imported plastics and support local economies while simultaneously addressing plastic pollution.

3. Reusable and Refillable Packaging Systems

Another innovative approach to reducing plastic consumption in SIDS is the implementation of reusable and refillable packaging systems. Instead of single-use plastic containers and packaging, consumers are encouraged to use durable, refillable containers that can be returned and refilled at designated collection points or refill stations. This not only reduces the amount of plastic waste generated but also promotes a shift towards a circular economy model, where resources are kept in use for as long as possible, maximizing their value and minimizing environmental impact.

4. Community-Led Recycling Programs

Community-led recycling programs are instrumental in tackling plastic pollution in SIDS. By engaging local residents in waste separation, collection, and recycling initiatives, these programs not only divert plastic waste from landfills and marine environments but also foster a sense of environmental responsibility and community pride. In some SIDS, innovative approaches such as incentivized recycling schemes, where participants receive rewards or discounts for recycling, have proven effective in encouraging participation and promoting sustainable behaviour change.

5. Upcycling and Creative Reuse

Upcycling, the process of transforming discarded materials into new and useful products, offers a creative solution to plastic pollution in SIDS. From turning plastic bottles into eco-friendly building materials to repurposing ocean debris into art installations, upcycling initiatives not only reduce plastic waste but also raise awareness about the value of recycling and inspire communities to rethink their relationship with disposable plastics. In SIDS, where resourcefulness and ingenuity are often integral parts of daily life, upcycling projects hold particular promise as a means of addressing plastic pollution while promoting cultural resilience and creativity.

6. Educational Campaigns and Outreach Programs

Effective solutions to plastic pollution in SIDS must go beyond technological innovations and policy interventions to include comprehensive education and outreach efforts. Educational campaigns aimed at raising awareness about the environmental impacts of plastic pollution, promoting sustainable consumption habits, and empowering communities to take action are essential components of any successful mitigation strategy. By equipping individuals with the knowledge and tools they need to make informed choices and advocate for change, educational initiatives can catalyse widespread behaviour change and lay the foundation for a more sustainable future.

Innovative solutions for sustainable alternatives to plastic are essential in the fight against plastic pollution in Small Island Developing States. By embracing biodegradable materials, harnessing local resources, promoting reusable packaging systems, empowering communities through recycling programs, fostering creative reuse initiatives, and investing in comprehensive education and outreach efforts, SIDS can reduce their plastic footprint, protect their natural environments, and build more resilient and sustainable communities for generations to come.

Community Engagement and Education

Community engagement and education are essential components of any successful plastic pollution mitigation strategy. By empowering local communities with knowledge and resources, SIDS are fostering a sense of ownership and collective responsibility for protecting their natural environments.

Engaging communities and fostering environmental literacy are essential components of any strategy aimed at mitigating plastic pollution in Small Island Developing States (SIDS). This chapter explores innovative approaches to community engagement and education, highlighting successful initiatives that empower local residents to become stewards of their environment and champions for sustainable practices.

1. Participatory Waste Management Programs

Traditional top-down approaches to waste management often fall short in SIDS due to limited resources and infrastructure. Innovative solutions leverage community participation to address this challenge. By involving residents in waste collection, sorting, and recycling efforts, these programs not only reduce the burden on formal waste management systems but also foster a sense of ownership and responsibility among community members.

2. Plastic-Free Schools and Youth Empowerment

Educating the next generation is key to building a sustainable future free from plastic pollution. Schools in SIDS can serve as catalysts for change by implementing plastic-free policies, integrating environmental education into the curriculum, and empowering students to take action through extracurricular activities such as beach cleanups, recycling drives, and advocacy campaigns.

3. Art and Creative Expression

Art has the power to inspire, provoke thought, and catalyse action. In SIDS, artists, activists, and community organizers are harnessing the creative arts to raise awareness about plastic pollution and spark conversations about solutions. From murals and sculptures made from recycled materials to multimedia installations and theatre performances, these artistic interventions engage people of all ages and backgrounds in meaningful dialogue about the environmental challenges facing their communities.

4. Digital Platforms and Social Media Campaigns

In an increasingly connected world, digital platforms and social media offer powerful tools for community engagement and education. SIDS organizations and grassroots initiatives are leveraging these platforms to disseminate information, share success stories, and mobilize support for plastic pollution mitigation efforts. Through interactive websites, online forums, and viral social media campaigns, they are reaching audiences far beyond their local communities and inspiring action on a global scale.

5. Traditional Knowledge and Cultural Heritage

Indigenous peoples and local communities in SIDS possess valuable traditional knowledge and cultural practices that can inform and enrich efforts to combat plastic pollution. By recognizing and honouring these traditions, initiatives can foster a deeper connection to the natural world and promote sustainable lifestyles rooted in respect for the environment. Incorporating traditional storytelling, ceremonies, and rituals into educational programs creates meaningful opportunities for intergenerational learning and cultural exchange.

6. Eco-Tourism and Sustainable Development

Tourism is a vital economic sector in many SIDS, but unchecked tourism development can exacerbate plastic pollution and environmental degradation. Innovative approaches to eco-tourism promote responsible travel practices, support local economies, and raise awareness about the importance of protecting fragile ecosystems. By offering eco-friendly accommodations, organizing eco-tours, and engaging tourists in conservation activities, these initiatives demonstrate that sustainable tourism can be both financially lucrative and environmentally sustainable.

7. Cross-Sector Collaboration and Partnership

Effective community engagement and education require collaboration across sectors and stakeholders, including government agencies, non-governmental organizations, businesses, academia, and local communities. By fostering partnerships and pooling resources, initiatives can maximize their impact, leverage expertise from diverse fields, and ensure that efforts are coordinated and sustainable in the long term.

Innovative solutions for community engagement and education are essential pillars of efforts to mitigate plastic pollution in Small Island Developing States. By empowering communities, fostering environmental literacy, and promoting sustainable practices, these initiatives create a foundation for lasting change and a brighter, cleaner future for generations to come.

Innovative solutions such as waste reduction and recycling programs, sustainable alternatives to plastic, and community engagement and education are essential for mitigating plastic pollution in Small Island Developing States. By harnessing the creativity, resilience, and collective action of their communities, SIDS are paving the way for a more sustainable and plastic-free future.

Chapter - 6
Case Studies from SIDS

Case Studies from SIDS

Drawing on real-world examples, this chapter highlights both successes and ongoing challenges in the fight against plastic pollution in SIDS. It offers valuable insights into the factors driving progress and the barriers that must be overcome.

In the battle against plastic pollution, Small Island Developing States (SIDS) have emerged as both laboratories for innovative solutions and frontline battlegrounds where the impacts of plastic waste are keenly felt. This chapter delves into various case studies from SIDS, showcasing both success stories and ongoing challenges, while distilling valuable lessons learned along the way.

Success Stories

In the battle against plastic pollution, Small Island Developing States (SIDS) have emerged as beacons of innovation and resilience, pioneering creative solutions to mitigate the impacts of plastic waste on their fragile ecosystems and communities. This chapter highlights a selection of success stories from various SIDS, showcasing inspiring examples of effective strategies and initiatives that have made a tangible difference in combating plastic pollution.

1. Seychelles: A Model for Marine Protection

The Seychelles, an archipelago nation in the Indian Ocean, has implemented ambitious measures to protect its marine environment from plastic pollution. Through collaboration between government agencies, non-governmental organizations (NGOs), and local communities, Seychelles has established marine protected areas and implemented strict regulations on single-use plastics. These efforts have led to significant reductions in plastic waste entering the ocean, preserving the pristine beauty of Seychelles' coral reefs and marine biodiversity.

2. Palau: Leading the Way in Plastic Bans

Palau, located in the western Pacific Ocean, has gained international recognition for its bold stance against plastic pollution. In 2020, Palau became the first country to ban sunscreen containing harmful chemicals that damage coral reefs, demonstrating its commitment to protecting marine ecosystems. Furthermore, Palau has implemented a ban on single-use plastic bags and styrofoam containers, encouraging the use of sustainable alternatives and promoting a culture of environmental stewardship among its citizens.

3. Jamaica: Empowering Communities for Clean Seas

Jamaica has adopted a grassroots approach to tackling plastic pollution, engaging local communities in cleanup efforts and waste management initiatives. Through partnerships with NGOs and government agencies, community-led cleanup campaigns have mobilized thousands of volunteers to remove plastic debris from beaches and coastal areas. These efforts have not only reduced plastic pollution but also fostered a sense of environmental responsibility and pride among Jamaican communities.

4. Maldives: Innovations in Waste Management

The Maldives, renowned for its picturesque islands and crystal-clear waters, faces unique challenges in managing waste due to its dispersed geography and limited land area. To address this, the Maldives has invested in innovative waste management solutions, including the establishment of waste-to-energy plants and the implementation of recycling programs. These initiatives have significantly reduced the amount of plastic waste ending up in landfills or polluting the ocean, paving the way for a more sustainable future for the Maldives.

5. Fiji: Promoting Sustainable Tourism Practices

Fiji, a popular tourist destination in the South Pacific, recognizes the importance of sustainable tourism in preserving its natural environment and combating plastic pollution. Through initiatives such as the "Fiji Plastic Free" campaign, hotels and resorts across Fiji have implemented measures to reduce single-use plastics and promote eco-friendly alternatives. These efforts have not only enhanced the visitor experience but also minimized the environmental footprint of tourism in Fiji, ensuring the long-term viability of its pristine landscapes and marine habitats.

6. Barbados: Harnessing Technology for Ocean Cleanup

Barbados has embraced technology as a tool for combating plastic pollution in its coastal waters. Through partnerships with research institutions and technology companies, Barbados has deployed innovative solutions such as autonomous drones and underwater robots to survey and remove plastic debris from its marine environment. These high-tech interventions complement traditional cleanup efforts and enable more efficient and targeted removal of plastic waste, helping to protect Barbados' marine biodiversity and coastal communities.

These success stories from Small Island Developing States demonstrate the power of collaboration, innovation, and community engagement in the fight against plastic pollution. By learning from these examples and scaling up successful strategies, SIDS and other coastal nations can continue to make progress towards a cleaner, healthier, and more sustainable future for our oceans and planet.

Ongoing Challenges

While progress has been made in addressing plastic pollution in Small Island Developing States (SIDS), significant challenges persist. This chapter explores in detail some of the ongoing challenges faced by SIDS in their efforts to mitigate plastic pollution, drawing on real-world case studies from various regions.

1. Limited Waste Management Infrastructure

Despite efforts to improve waste management systems, many SIDS still lack adequate infrastructure for collecting, sorting, and processing plastic waste. In some cases, remote island communities face logistical challenges in transporting waste to central disposal facilities, leading to accumulation in coastal areas and natural habitats.

Case Study: Maldives

The Maldives, known for its stunning beaches and pristine marine environment, faces significant challenges in managing plastic waste due to its dispersed island geography. While initiatives such as waste collection programs and recycling facilities exist in urban centres, remote islands often struggle to access these services, leading to pollution of coastal ecosystems.

2. Dependency on Imported Goods and Packaging

SIDS often rely heavily on imported goods, many of which come packaged in single-use plastics. This dependency exacerbates the challenge of plastic pollution, as recycling facilities may be insufficient to handle the volume of waste generated. Additionally, efforts to promote alternatives to plastic packaging face resistance from consumers and businesses accustomed to convenience and cost-effectiveness.

Case Study: Fiji

In Fiji, a significant portion of consumer goods, including food and beverages, is imported and packaged in plastic. While initiatives to promote reusable alternatives and reduce packaging waste have been implemented, progress is hindered by the prevalence of single-use plastics in everyday life and the limited availability of recycling facilities outside urban centres.

3. Lack of Public Awareness and Education

Despite increased attention to plastic pollution globally, public awareness and education remain limited in many SIDS. Misconceptions about waste disposal practices, coupled with a lack of understanding of the environmental impacts of plastic pollution, contribute to continued littering and improper waste management behaviours.

Case Study: Jamaica

In Jamaica, efforts to raise public awareness about plastic pollution have encountered challenges due to competing priorities and resource constraints. While educational campaigns targeting schools and communities have been launched, sustaining momentum and behaviour change remains a long-term challenge.

4. Economic Constraints and Resource Limitations

SIDS often face economic constraints and limited resources, which can impede the implementation of comprehensive plastic pollution mitigation strategies. Investments in waste management infrastructure, recycling facilities, and research and development of sustainable alternatives may be prioritized lower amid competing demands for healthcare, education, and infrastructure development.

Case Study: Vanuatu

Vanuatu, an archipelago in the South Pacific, grapples with limited financial resources and capacity constraints in addressing plastic pollution. While community-based initiatives and partnerships with NGOs have yielded some progress, the scale of the challenge requires sustained investment and support from both domestic and international stakeholders.

5. Climate Change and Natural Disasters

Climate change exacerbates the impacts of plastic pollution in SIDS, with rising sea levels, extreme weather events, and erosion threatening coastal habitats and exacerbating plastic debris accumulation. Natural disasters such as hurricanes and cyclones can disrupt waste management systems and exacerbate pollution, further compounding the challenges faced by SIDS.

Case Study: Seychelles

The Seychelles, an island nation in the Indian Ocean, is highly vulnerable to the impacts of climate change and extreme weather events. Plastic pollution is exacerbated during cyclone seasons, as flooding and storm surges disperse plastic waste across coastal areas, hampering cleanup efforts and posing risks to marine biodiversity.

Despite these challenges, SIDS are resilient and resourceful in their efforts to tackle plastic pollution. By addressing these ongoing challenges through innovative solutions, strengthened partnerships, and community engagement, SIDS can pave the way towards a more sustainable and resilient future for their islands and the planet as a whole.

Lessons Learned

In the battle against plastic pollution, Small Island Developing States (SIDS) have emerged as both laboratories for innovative solutions and frontline communities grappling with the dire consequences of plastic waste. This chapter delves into case studies from various SIDS, highlighting the lessons learned, successes achieved, and ongoing challenges faced in their efforts to mitigate plastic pollution.

1. The Bahamas: A Paradigm Shift in Waste Management

➢ **Lesson Learned:**

The Bahamas has undergone a significant transformation in waste management practices, shifting from reliance on landfill disposal to embracing recycling and sustainable waste management initiatives.

➢ **Successes:**

Implementation of recycling programs, community engagement campaigns, and legislative measures to ban single-use plastics have yielded tangible results in reducing plastic pollution.

➤ Challenges:

Limited infrastructure and financial resources pose ongoing challenges to expanding recycling capabilities and ensuring widespread adoption of sustainable practices.

2. Seychelles: Mobilizing Multi-sectoral Collaboration

➤ Lesson Learned:

Seychelles has demonstrated the importance of multi-sectoral collaboration in addressing plastic pollution, involving government agencies, NGOs, businesses, and local communities.

➤ Successes:

Collaborative efforts have led to the development of comprehensive marine protection policies, establishment of marine protected areas, and implementation of education and outreach programs.

➤ **Challenges:**

Maintaining momentum and coordination among diverse stakeholders remains a challenge, particularly in the face of limited resources and competing priorities.

3. Fiji: Harnessing Traditional Knowledge and Community Empowerment

➤ **Lesson Learned:**

Fiji has leveraged traditional knowledge and community-based approaches to tackle plastic pollution, recognizing the cultural and ecological significance of local practices.

➤ **Successes:**

Initiatives such as traditional Fijian village clean-up campaigns, mangrove restoration projects, and sustainable fishing practices have fostered a sense of ownership and stewardship among communities.

➤ **Challenges:**

Balancing traditional practices with modern development pressures, addressing plastic pollution in remote and underserved communities, and ensuring equitable participation and benefits for all stakeholders are ongoing challenges.

4. Barbados: Integrating Plastic Pollution Mitigation into Tourism Strategies

➤ Lesson Learned:

Barbados has integrated plastic pollution mitigation into its tourism strategies, recognizing the importance of preserving pristine environments to sustain the tourism industry.

➤ Successes:

Implementation of beach clean-up initiatives, promotion of eco-friendly tourism practices, and partnerships with hotels and resorts to reduce plastic use have contributed to cleaner beaches and enhanced visitor experiences.

➤ Challenges:

Balancing environmental conservation with economic development objectives, addressing plastic pollution generated by tourism activities, and ensuring compliance with sustainability standards are ongoing priorities.

5. Maldives: Embracing Innovative Technologies for Waste Management

➤ Lesson Learned:

The Maldives has embraced innovative technologies for waste management, harnessing solar-powered recycling machines, 3D printing from recycled plastic, and mobile applications for waste collection and monitoring.

➤ Successes:

Adoption of technology-driven solutions has improved waste collection efficiency, reduced reliance on landfill disposal, and empowered communities to actively participate in waste management efforts.

➤ Challenges:

Scaling up technology deployment, ensuring affordability and accessibility of solutions, and addressing the digital divide in remote island communities are ongoing challenges.

6. Tonga: Strengthening Regional Collaboration for Plastic Pollution Mitigation

➢ Lesson Learned:

Tonga has emphasized the importance of regional collaboration in addressing plastic pollution, leveraging partnerships with neighbouring SIDS, regional organizations, and international donors.

➢ Successes:

Participation in regional forums such as the Pacific Islands Forum and the Pacific Ocean Alliance has facilitated knowledge sharing, resource mobilization, and coordinated action on plastic pollution.

➢ Challenges:

Navigating geopolitical dynamics, aligning diverse interests and priorities, and sustaining momentum for collective action amidst competing demands pose ongoing challenges to regional collaboration efforts.

The case studies from SIDS presented in this chapter underscore the diversity of approaches, contexts, and challenges in the fight against plastic pollution. From innovative waste management solutions to community-based initiatives and regional collaborations, these examples offer valuable insights and inspiration for policymakers, practitioners, and advocates working to mitigate plastic pollution in SIDS and beyond. By learning from the experiences of these frontline communities, we can chart a course towards a cleaner, healthier, and more resilient future for our oceans and planet.

Chapter - 7
The Role of Technology

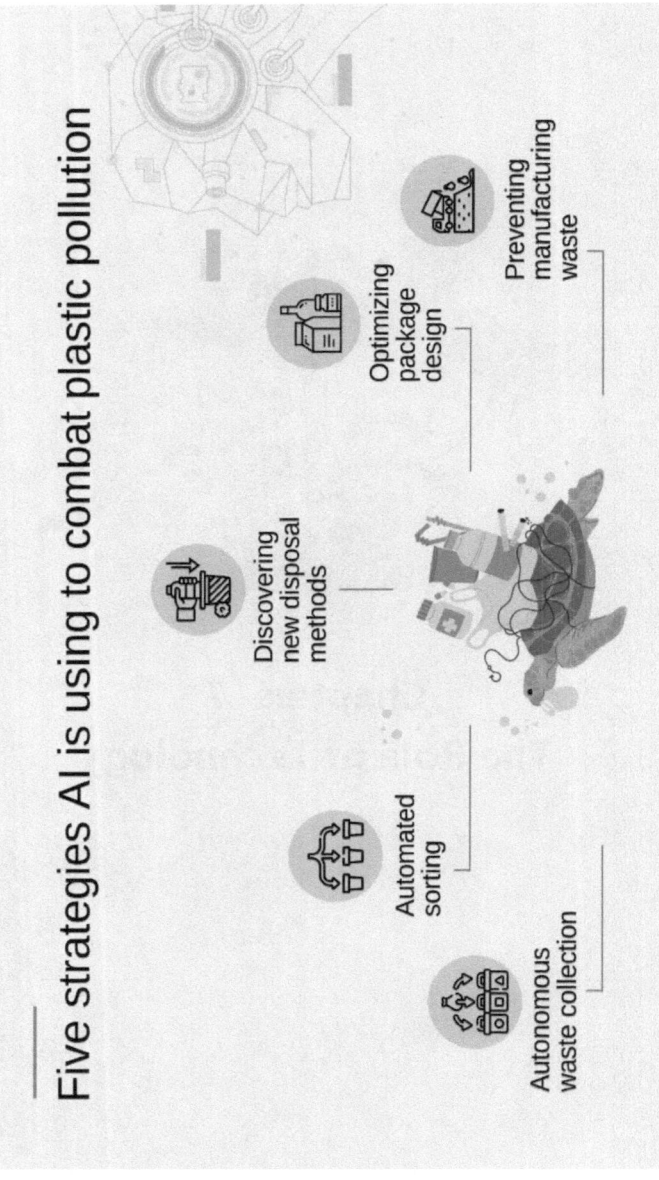

The Role of Technology

Technology holds immense potential in the battle against plastic pollution. This chapter explores how innovations in monitoring, detection, and cleanup technologies are revolutionizing our approach to tackling plastic waste in marine environments.

Technology has emerged as a critical ally in the fight against plastic pollution, offering innovative solutions to monitor, detect, and clean up marine debris. In Small Island Developing States (SIDS), where the impacts of plastic pollution are particularly acute, leveraging technology effectively can make a significant difference in mitigating this environmental threat.

Monitoring and Detection Systems

One of the first steps in addressing plastic pollution is understanding its scope and distribution. Monitoring and detection systems provide invaluable insights into the sources, pathways, and accumulation of marine debris. In SIDS, where vast oceanic expanses often mask the extent of pollution, these systems play a crucial role in guiding targeted intervention strategies.

In the battle against plastic pollution, technology serves as a powerful ally, offering innovative solutions for monitoring, detecting, and ultimately mitigating the impacts of plastic waste in Small Island Developing States (SIDS). This chapter explores the diverse array of technological tools and approaches that are revolutionizing our ability to understand, track, and address plastic pollution in SIDS environments.

1. Remote Sensing Technologies

Remote sensing technologies, including satellite imagery and aerial drones, play a crucial role in monitoring and detecting plastic pollution in SIDS. Satellites equipped with high-resolution sensors can capture detailed images of coastal areas, allowing scientists to identify and quantify floating debris and coastal litter. Aerial drones provide an additional layer of precision, enabling researchers to survey hard-to-reach areas and map plastic hotspots with unprecedented accuracy.

2. Automated Image Analysis

The sheer volume of data generated by remote sensing technologies necessitates advanced image analysis techniques to extract meaningful insights. Machine learning algorithms and computer vision systems can automatically identify and classify plastic debris in satellite and drone imagery, streamlining the data analysis process and facilitating rapid response efforts. By leveraging artificial intelligence, researchers can detect subtle patterns and trends in plastic pollution dynamics, informing targeted intervention strategies.

3. Sensor Networks

In-situ sensor networks offer real-time monitoring capabilities, providing continuous data streams on water quality, marine debris concentrations, and other environmental parameters. Buoy-mounted sensors equipped with cameras, spectrometers, and hydrophones can detect and characterize floating plastics, enabling early warning systems for plastic pollution events and facilitating timely intervention measures. By integrating sensor networks into existing marine observation networks, SIDS can enhance their capacity to monitor and manage plastic pollution in coastal waters.

4. Citizen Science Platforms

Citizen science platforms harness the collective power of volunteers to collect, analyse, and share data on plastic pollution in SIDS. Mobile applications and online portals enable citizens to report plastic debris sightings, participate in cleanup efforts, and contribute to scientific research initiatives. By engaging local communities in data collection and monitoring activities, SIDS can foster greater environmental awareness and empower citizens to take ownership of plastic pollution mitigation efforts.

5. Blockchain Technology

Blockchain technology offers a transparent and tamper-proof system for tracking plastic waste along the supply chain. By assigning unique digital identities to plastic products and packaging materials, blockchain platforms enable traceability and accountability throughout the product lifecycle. SIDS can leverage blockchain solutions to monitor the movement of plastic waste, verify recycling and disposal practices, and incentivize sustainable consumption and production behaviours among businesses and consumers.

6. Integrated Data Platforms

Integrating data from multiple sources into centralized platforms enhances the effectiveness of plastic pollution monitoring and management efforts. Geographic information systems (GIS) enable spatial analysis and visualization of plastic pollution hotspots, facilitating targeted intervention strategies and resource allocation. By combining satellite imagery, sensor data, citizen science reports, and other sources of information, SIDS can gain comprehensive insights into the drivers and impacts of plastic pollution in their coastal environments.

7. Capacity Building and Technology Transfer

Building local capacity in the use of technology for plastic pollution monitoring and detection is essential for long-term sustainability. Training programs, workshops, and knowledge-sharing initiatives can empower SIDS researchers, policymakers, and practitioners to leverage cutting-edge technologies effectively. Additionally, technology transfer partnerships with developed countries and international organizations can facilitate access to state-of-the-art equipment, software, and expertise, enabling SIDS to build resilient and adaptive plastic pollution monitoring systems.

Thus, it can be observed that technology holds immense promise in the fight against plastic pollution in Small Island Developing States. From remote sensing and automated image analysis to sensor networks and citizen science platforms, innovative technologies are transforming our understanding of plastic pollution dynamics and informing targeted intervention strategies. By harnessing the power of technology, SIDS can enhance their capacity to monitor, detect, and mitigate plastic pollution, safeguarding their marine environments and promoting sustainable development for future generations.

Ocean Cleanup Technologies

Removing existing plastic waste from the marine environment is a daunting task, but advances in ocean cleanup technologies offer promising solutions to this challenge. From passive drifters to active collection systems, these technologies are designed to intercept and remove plastic debris from the ocean before it causes further harm.

➤ Passive Drifters:

Floating booms and barriers utilize ocean currents to passively collect plastic debris, effectively channelling it towards collection points where it can be retrieved and recycled. These low-cost, low-maintenance systems are particularly well-suited for deployment in coastal areas and estuaries where plastic pollution accumulates.

➤ Active Collection Systems:

Autonomous surface vessels equipped with onboard sensors and robotic arms can actively patrol marine environments and collect plastic debris. These advanced systems leverage artificial intelligence and machine learning algorithms to navigate complex oceanic terrain and target areas of high plastic concentration.

➢ **Innovative Materials:**

Research into biodegradable and bio-based materials offers potential solutions for mitigating plastic pollution at its source. By developing alternative materials that break down harmlessly in the marine environment, scientists are exploring new avenues for reducing the long-term impact of plastic waste.

Data-driven Approaches

Harnessing the power of data is essential for developing effective strategies to combat plastic pollution in SIDS. By leveraging data-driven approaches, policymakers, scientists, and stakeholders can identify priority areas for intervention, track progress over time, and measure the effectiveness of mitigation efforts.

➤ Integrated Data Platforms:

Centralized data platforms facilitate the collection, analysis, and sharing of information on plastic pollution across multiple stakeholders. These platforms enable real-time collaboration and decision-making, ensuring that resources are allocated efficiently and interventions are targeted where they are needed most.

➤ Predictive Modelling:

Predictive modelling techniques allow researchers to forecast future trends in plastic pollution based on historical data and environmental variables. By anticipating changes in plastic distribution patterns and ecosystem impacts, decision-makers can proactively adapt strategies to mitigate emerging threats.

➤ Public Awareness Campaigns:

Utilizing data visualization tools and interactive maps, public awareness campaigns can raise awareness about plastic pollution and engage citizens in conservation efforts. By translating complex scientific data into accessible formats, these campaigns empower individuals to take action and advocate for change.

Incorporating advanced monitoring and detection systems, ocean cleanup technologies, and data-driven approaches into plastic pollution mitigation efforts in Small Island Developing States holds the promise of a cleaner, healthier marine environment for current and future generations. By embracing innovation and collaboration, SIDS can lead the way towards a sustainable future free from the scourge of plastic pollution.

Chapter - 8
Building Resilience

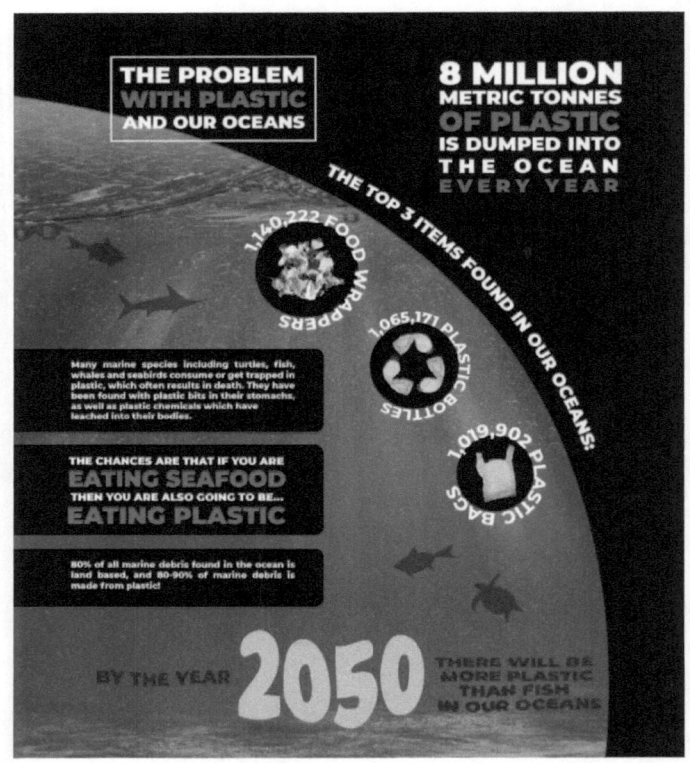

Building Resilience

Plastic pollution is not an isolated issue but is intricately linked to broader challenges such as climate change and sustainable development. This chapter examines strategies for building resilience in SIDS and integrating plastic pollution mitigation into long-term planning efforts.

Small Island Developing States (SIDS) face a myriad of challenges, from the existential threat of climate change to the pervasive scourge of plastic pollution. Building resilience in these vulnerable regions requires a multifaceted approach that integrates adaptation strategies for climate change with efforts to mitigate plastic pollution, all within the framework of sustainable development goals (SDGs). This chapter explores the interconnectedness of these issues and outlines strategies for building resilience in SIDS communities.

Adapting to Climate Change

Small Island Developing States (SIDS) face unique and acute challenges posed by climate change. Rising sea levels, increased frequency and intensity of extreme weather events, ocean acidification, and coral bleaching are just some of the consequences that threaten the very existence of these vulnerable nations. In the context of mitigating plastic pollution, building resilience to climate change is not only essential for safeguarding ecosystems and livelihoods but also for enhancing the effectiveness of efforts to address plastic waste. This chapter explores the interconnectedness between climate change adaptation and plastic pollution mitigation in SIDS, highlighting strategies for building resilience in the face of these converging challenges.

Understanding the Climate Change Challenge in SIDS

SIDS are among the most exposed and vulnerable to the impacts of climate change due to their geographical location, small land area, and limited resources. The effects of climate change, such as sea-level rise and changes in weather patterns, exacerbate existing vulnerabilities, including those related to plastic pollution. Understanding the specific risks and vulnerabilities faced by SIDS is crucial for developing targeted adaptation strategies.

Integrating Climate Change Adaptation and Plastic Pollution Mitigation

Adaptation to climate change and mitigation of plastic pollution are often treated as separate issues. However, they are deeply interconnected, with many adaptation measures also contributing to plastic pollution reduction and vice versa. For example, restoring coastal ecosystems such as mangroves and coral reefs not only helps mitigate climate change impacts but also provides natural barriers against plastic pollution.

Nature-Based Solutions for Resilience

Nature-based solutions offer cost-effective and sustainable approaches to building resilience in SIDS. Restoring and conserving coastal ecosystems, such as mangroves, seagrass beds, and coral reefs, can provide multiple benefits, including protection against storm surges, erosion, and plastic pollution. Additionally, these ecosystems sequester carbon and support biodiversity, enhancing overall ecosystem health and resilience.

Enhancing Infrastructure and Disaster Preparedness

Investments in resilient infrastructure and disaster preparedness are essential for reducing the impacts of climate change and plastic pollution in SIDS. Building seawalls, elevating buildings, and implementing early warning systems can help minimize the risks of coastal erosion, flooding, and storm damage. Strengthening waste management systems and improving recycling and waste-to-energy infrastructure can also reduce plastic pollution and enhance community resilience.

Community-Based Adaptation and Empowerment

Community participation and empowerment are critical components of climate change adaptation and plastic pollution mitigation efforts in SIDS. Engaging local communities in decision-making processes, building capacity for sustainable resource management, and promoting traditional knowledge and practices can enhance the effectiveness and sustainability of adaptation initiatives. Furthermore, fostering partnerships between governments, civil society organizations, and the private sector can mobilize resources and support community-led adaptation actions.

Mainstreaming Climate Change Adaptation and Plastic Pollution Mitigation

Mainstreaming climate change adaptation and plastic pollution mitigation into national policies, plans, and development strategies is essential for long-term resilience in SIDS. Integrating climate resilience considerations into coastal zone management, land-use planning, and disaster risk reduction frameworks can help ensure that adaptation measures are prioritized and effectively implemented. Similarly, incorporating plastic pollution reduction targets and initiatives into national waste management plans and environmental policies can help address the interconnected challenges of climate change and plastic pollution.

Adaptation strategies are essential for enhancing the resilience of SIDS communities in the face of these challenges. Key elements of adaptation include:

1. Enhancing Coastal Protection:

Given their low-lying topography, many SIDS are particularly susceptible to the impacts of sea-level rise and coastal erosion. Investing in natural infrastructure such as mangroves and coral reefs can help buffer coastlines against erosion and storm surges.

2. Building Climate-Resilient Infrastructure:

Infrastructure development must take into account the projected impacts of climate change, including increased flooding and saltwater intrusion. Retrofitting existing infrastructure and incorporating climate resilience measures into new construction can help minimize vulnerability.

3. Diversifying Livelihoods:

SIDS economies are often heavily reliant on sectors such as tourism and fisheries, which are vulnerable to climate change impacts. Diversifying livelihoods through sustainable agriculture, renewable energy development, and eco-tourism can enhance resilience and reduce dependence on climate-sensitive industries.

4. Strengthening Disaster Preparedness and Response:

Investing in early warning systems, disaster preparedness training, and community resilience-building initiatives can improve SIDS' ability to anticipate and respond to climate-related disasters, saving lives and minimizing economic losses.

5. Fostering Regional Collaboration:

Many climate change impacts transcend national boundaries, making regional cooperation essential for effective adaptation. SIDS can leverage regional platforms and partnerships to share knowledge, resources, and best practices for climate resilience.

Building resilience to climate change is a complex and multifaceted challenge that requires coordinated action at the local, national, regional, and global levels. By integrating climate change adaptation and plastic pollution mitigation efforts,

SIDS can enhance their resilience to the impacts of climate change while simultaneously reducing plastic pollution and promoting sustainable development. Through nature-based solutions, infrastructure improvements, community empowerment, and policy mainstreaming, SIDS can pave the way toward a more resilient and sustainable future for current and future generations.

Integrating Plastic Pollution Mitigation into Sustainable Development Goals

Plastic pollution poses a significant threat to the sustainable development of Small Island Developing States (SIDS), undermining their environmental integrity, economic stability, and social well-being. In response, SIDS are increasingly recognizing the importance of integrating plastic pollution mitigation into their broader sustainable development agendas. This chapter explores the synergies between plastic pollution mitigation efforts and the Sustainable Development Goals (SDGs), highlighting the opportunities for building resilience in SIDS.

1. Understanding the Interconnectedness of Plastic Pollution and Sustainable Development

Plastic pollution is not just an environmental issue; it is intricately linked to multiple dimensions of sustainable development. From Goal 14 (Life Below Water) to Goal 12 (Responsible Consumption and Production), addressing plastic pollution intersects with various SDGs, including poverty eradication, health, education, and climate action. Recognizing these interconnections is essential for crafting holistic and effective strategies for sustainable development in SIDS.

2. Integrating Plastic Pollution Mitigation into National Development Plans

Many SIDS have developed national development plans that align with the SDGs. By integrating plastic pollution mitigation into these plans, countries can mainstream efforts to address plastic pollution across sectors such as waste management, tourism, fisheries, and education. This entails setting specific targets, allocating resources, and establishing monitoring mechanisms to track progress towards reducing plastic pollution while advancing sustainable development objectives.

3. Fostering Multi-Stakeholder Collaboration

Building resilience requires collaborative action across governments, civil society, academia, and the private sector. SIDS can leverage existing platforms and partnerships, such as national sustainable development councils and regional alliances, to foster dialogue, share best practices, and mobilize resources for plastic pollution mitigation initiatives. Engaging stakeholders at all levels ensures that interventions are contextually relevant, inclusive, and sustainable.

4. Promoting Circular Economy Approaches

Transitioning towards a circular economy is central to addressing plastic pollution and promoting sustainable development in SIDS. By redesigning products, promoting reuse and recycling, and investing in waste-to-energy technologies, SIDS can minimize the generation of plastic waste and maximize the value of resources. Circular economy principles not only reduce environmental impacts but also stimulate innovation, create green jobs, and enhance economic resilience.

5. Strengthening Resilience to Climate Change Impacts

Plastic pollution exacerbates the impacts of climate change on SIDS, with marine plastic debris acting as vectors for invasive species and pollutants. By mitigating plastic pollution, SIDS can enhance their resilience to climate change impacts, such as sea-level rise, ocean acidification, and extreme weather events. Additionally, promoting sustainable waste management practices contributes to greenhouse gas mitigation efforts, further aligning with SDG 13 (Climate Action).

6. Empowering Communities through Education and Awareness

Education and awareness-raising are essential components of building resilience to plastic pollution in SIDS. By incorporating environmental education into school curricula, raising public awareness through campaigns and outreach initiatives, and fostering community participation in waste management programs, SIDS can empower citizens to become agents of change. Education not only instils a sense of environmental stewardship but also fosters sustainable behaviours and attitudes.

7. Monitoring, Evaluation, and Adaptive Management

Effective monitoring, evaluation, and adaptive management are critical for ensuring the success of plastic pollution mitigation efforts in SIDS. By establishing robust monitoring systems, collecting data on plastic pollution trends and impacts, and regularly evaluating the effectiveness of interventions, SIDS can identify emerging challenges, adjust strategies accordingly, and improve decision-making processes over time.

8. Leveraging International Support and Financing Mechanisms

International support and financing mechanisms play a crucial role in assisting SIDS in their efforts to address plastic pollution and achieve sustainable development goals. SIDS can access funding through international organizations, such as the Global Environment Facility (GEF) and the Green Climate Fund (GCF), to implement plastic pollution mitigation projects and build institutional capacity. Additionally, leveraging South-South cooperation and knowledge exchange facilitates peer learning and enhances SIDS' collective resilience.

Integrating plastic pollution mitigation into sustainable development goals is critical for building resilience and promoting holistic, inclusive development. Key strategies include:

1. Promoting Circular Economy Principles:

Transitioning to a circular economy model, where resources are reused, recycled, and repurposed, can help minimize the generation of plastic waste and reduce reliance on finite natural resources. SIDS can incentivize circular economy practices through policy incentives and public-private partnerships.

2. Strengthening Waste Management Systems:

Improving waste management infrastructure, including collection, recycling, and disposal facilities, is essential for reducing plastic pollution in SIDS. Investing in decentralized waste management solutions tailored to local contexts can improve efficiency and accessibility.

3. Raising Awareness and Changing Behaviours:

Education and public awareness campaigns play a crucial role in changing consumer attitudes and behaviours towards plastic consumption and disposal. SIDS governments, civil society organizations, and the private sector can collaborate to develop targeted messaging and outreach programs.

4. Supporting Innovation and Research:

Investing in research and innovation can drive the development of sustainable alternatives to single-use plastics and packaging. SIDS can support local entrepreneurs and innovators through funding opportunities, incubator programs, and technology transfer initiatives.

5. Mainstreaming Plastic Pollution Mitigation in Policy and Planning:

Integrating plastic pollution mitigation goals into national development plans, environmental policies, and sectoral strategies can ensure that efforts to address plastic pollution are prioritized and coordinated across government agencies and stakeholders.

By integrating adaptation strategies for climate change with efforts to mitigate plastic pollution and advancing progress towards sustainable development goals, SIDS can build resilience, foster inclusive growth, and safeguard the well-being of present and future generations.

In the face of formidable challenges, building resilience in Small Island Developing States requires a comprehensive, integrated approach that addresses the interconnected threats of climate change and plastic pollution while advancing sustainable development goals. By leveraging regional cooperation, fostering innovation, and empowering local communities, SIDS can chart a course towards a more resilient, sustainable future.

Integrating plastic pollution mitigation into sustainable development goals is not only essential for safeguarding the environment and promoting human well-being but also for building resilience in Small Island Developing States. By adopting a holistic approach that addresses the interconnected challenges of plastic pollution, climate change, and sustainable development, SIDS can chart a course towards a more resilient and prosperous future for generations to come.

Chapter - 9
Partnerships and Collaborations

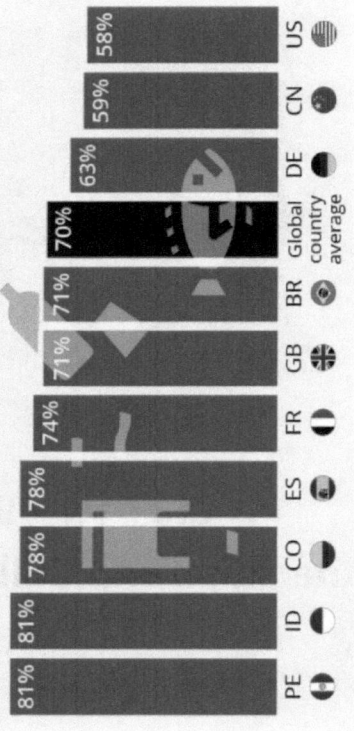

Partnerships and Collaborations

Addressing plastic pollution requires concerted action across sectors and stakeholders. This chapter explores the role of partnerships and collaborations in mobilizing resources, sharing knowledge, and driving collective action on a global scale.

Addressing plastic pollution in Small Island Developing States (SIDS) requires collaborative efforts across various sectors and stakeholders. Partnerships between governmental and non-governmental organizations (NGOs), private sector entities, and civil society are essential for mobilizing resources, sharing expertise, and implementing effective solutions. This chapter explores the multifaceted nature of partnerships and collaborations in mitigating plastic pollution in SIDS.

Governmental and Non-Governmental Organizations (NGOs)

Partnerships and collaborations between governmental and non-governmental organizations (NGOs) play a vital role in addressing the complex challenge of plastic pollution in Small Island Developing States (SIDS). By pooling resources, expertise, and knowledge, these partnerships foster innovation, amplify impact, and facilitate the implementation of comprehensive solutions. This chapter examines the diverse array of partnerships and collaborations that are driving progress in the fight against plastic pollution in SIDS.

Governmental Partnerships

Governments in SIDS recognize the urgent need to tackle plastic pollution and are increasingly forging partnerships with international organizations, neighbouring countries, and regional bodies to strengthen their response efforts. These partnerships focus on policy development, capacity building, and the implementation of sustainable waste management practices.

1. International Cooperation:

SIDS governments collaborate with international organizations such as the United Nations Environment Programme (UNEP), the World Bank, and the European Union to access technical assistance, funding, and expertise. Through initiatives like the Global Environment Facility (GEF) and the Clean Seas campaign, SIDS governments receive support for developing national action plans, implementing waste management infrastructure projects, and raising awareness about the impacts of plastic pollution.

2. Regional Alliances:

Regional organizations such as the Pacific Islands Forum (PIF), the Caribbean Community (CARICOM), and the Indian Ocean Commission (IOC) serve as platforms for SIDS governments to share best practices, harmonize policies, and coordinate regional initiatives to combat plastic pollution. These alliances facilitate joint research efforts, capacity-building workshops, and the development of regional waste management strategies tailored to the unique challenges of SIDS.

3. South-South Cooperation:

SIDS governments engage in South-South cooperation initiatives with other developing countries to exchange knowledge and expertise in waste management, recycling technologies, and community engagement strategies. Through partnerships with countries like Brazil, India, and Indonesia, SIDS governments learn from successful experiences and adapt innovative solutions to their local contexts.

Non-Governmental Partnerships

NGOs play a crucial role in mobilizing grassroots support, raising awareness, and implementing on-the-ground projects to reduce plastic pollution in SIDS. These organizations collaborate with governments, local communities, and international donors to drive change at both the local and global levels.

1. Community Engagement:

NGOs work closely with local communities in SIDS to raise awareness about the environmental impacts of plastic pollution, promote behaviour change, and empower communities to take action. Through education programs, beach cleanups, and sustainable livelihood initiatives, NGOs foster a sense of ownership and stewardship among residents, driving long-term sustainability efforts.

2. Corporate Partnerships:

NGOs collaborate with corporations to promote corporate social responsibility (CSR) initiatives, develop sustainable packaging solutions, and support circular economy models. Partnerships between NGOs and companies in industries such as tourism, hospitality, and consumer goods result in innovative projects that reduce plastic use, promote recycling, and minimize environmental footprint.

3. Research and Innovation:

NGOs partner with academic institutions, research organizations, and technology companies to conduct research on plastic pollution, develop innovative cleanup technologies, and advance scientific understanding of marine ecosystems. These partnerships contribute valuable data, insights, and solutions to inform policy decisions and guide conservation efforts in SIDS.

4. Advocacy and Policy Influence:

NGOs advocate for stronger regulations, policies, and incentives to address plastic pollution at the local, national, and international levels. Through partnerships with government agencies, advocacy coalitions, and civil society networks, NGOs amplify their voice, mobilize support, and influence policy outcomes to create an enabling environment for sustainable waste management practices in SIDS.

Case Study: The Caribbean Plastic Pollution Alliance (CaPPA)

CaPPA is a collaborative initiative launched by Caribbean governments, NGOs, and regional partners to address plastic pollution in the Caribbean Sea. Through coordinated action, CaPPA aims to reduce plastic waste, promote recycling, and protect marine ecosystems across the region. Key components of CaPPA's strategy include:

- Developing a regional action plan for plastic pollution reduction, aligned with international agreements such as the Caribbean Regional Action Plan on Marine Litter.

- Implementing community-based projects to reduce plastic use, improve waste management infrastructure, and raise awareness about marine conservation.

- Partnering with corporate stakeholders to promote sustainable packaging alternatives, support green businesses, and implement extended producer responsibility (EPR) schemes.

- Collaborating with international organizations, research institutions, and civil society groups to share knowledge, best practices, and resources for effective plastic pollution mitigation in the Caribbean.

Through the collective efforts of governments, NGOs, and other stakeholders, CaPPA exemplifies the power of partnerships in driving positive change and building resilience against plastic pollution in SIDS.

The above details underscores the importance of partnerships and collaborations between governmental and non-governmental stakeholders in addressing plastic pollution in Small Island Developing States. By working together across sectors and borders, we can leverage our collective strengths and resources to create a more sustainable and resilient future for SIDS and the global community.

Private Sector Engagement

Private sector engagement is integral to the success of efforts to mitigate plastic pollution in Small Island Developing States (SIDS). By leveraging the resources, expertise, and innovation of businesses, meaningful partnerships can be forged to drive sustainable solutions and catalyse positive change. This chapter explores the role of the private sector in addressing plastic pollution in SIDS, highlighting key partnerships, collaborative initiatives, and best practices.

The Importance of Private Sector Engagement

The private sector plays a critical role in the production, distribution, and consumption of plastics, making it a key stakeholder in efforts to combat plastic pollution. Businesses have a vested interest in protecting the environment and ensuring the long-term viability of their operations, making sustainability initiatives both a moral imperative and a strategic necessity. By engaging with the private sector, governments, NGOs, and other stakeholders can tap into resources, technologies, and networks that can accelerate progress towards a circular economy and a plastic-free future.

Types of Private Sector Partnerships

Private sector partnerships for plastic pollution mitigation in SIDS can take various forms, including:

1. Corporate Social Responsibility (CSR) Initiatives:

Many businesses have established CSR programs focused on environmental sustainability, including initiatives to reduce plastic waste, promote recycling, and support community-based conservation projects.

2. Industry Coalitions and Alliances:
Industry-led coalitions and alliances bring together companies from across sectors to collaborate on shared sustainability goals, such as reducing plastic packaging, developing alternative materials, and improving waste management practices.

3. Supply Chain Collaboration:
Collaboration along the entire supply chain, from manufacturers to retailers to consumers, is essential for addressing plastic pollution. Businesses can work together to redesign products, optimize packaging, and implement take-back and recycling programs.

4. Innovation and Technology Partnerships:
Collaboration between the private sector, research institutions, and government agencies can drive innovation in plastic alternatives, recycling

technologies, and waste management solutions tailored to the unique challenges faced by SIDS.

Best Practices for Private Sector Engagement

Successful private sector engagement in plastic pollution mitigation requires a commitment to transparency, accountability, and shared value creation. Key best practices include:

- **Setting Clear Goals and Targets:** Establishing measurable targets for plastic waste reduction, recycling rates, and sustainable sourcing can provide a roadmap for action and accountability.

- **Stakeholder Engagement:** Engaging with local communities, NGOs, government agencies, and other stakeholders is essential for building trust, understanding local needs, and co-creating solutions that are culturally and environmentally appropriate.

- **Investing in Innovation:** Investing in research and development of sustainable materials, technologies, and business models can drive long-term competitive advantage while reducing environmental impact.

- **Collaborative Advocacy:** Working together to advocate for policy reforms, industry standards, and regulatory incentives that support sustainable practices and level the playing field for responsible businesses.

Case Studies of Private Sector Partnerships in SIDS

1. Plastic-Free Packaging Initiatives:

Collaboration between tourism operators, retailers, and packaging manufacturers in Caribbean SIDS to reduce single-use plastics in the hospitality sector.

2. Waste Management Partnerships:

Public-private partnerships for the development of integrated waste management systems, including collection, sorting, recycling, and composting facilities, in Pacific Island nations.

3. Corporate Conservation Partnerships:

Collaboration between multinational corporations and local conservation organizations to support marine conservation initiatives, including beach clean-ups, coral reef restoration, and sustainable fisheries management.

Challenges and Opportunities

While private sector engagement holds great promise for addressing plastic pollution in SIDS, there are also challenges to overcome, including:

- Ensuring that partnerships are inclusive, equitable, and respectful of local communities and indigenous rights.

- Balancing short-term economic interests with long-term environmental sustainability.

- Overcoming regulatory barriers, market distortions, and information asymmetries that hinder progress.

- Scaling up successful initiatives and replicating best practices across industries and regions.

By harnessing the collective power of government, civil society, and the private sector, SIDS can overcome these challenges and chart a course towards a future where plastic pollution is a thing of the past, and the beauty and bounty of their natural environments are preserved for generations to come.

Hence, the above highlights the critical role of private sector engagement in addressing plastic pollution in Small Island Developing States, showcasing examples of successful partnerships and collaborative initiatives while also recognizing the challenges and opportunities that lie ahead.

Civil Society and Community Participation

Partnerships and collaborations between civil society organizations, local communities, and other stakeholders are essential components of effective plastic pollution mitigation efforts in Small Island Developing States (SIDS). This chapter explores the vital role that civil society and community participation play in addressing plastic pollution, highlighting successful initiatives, and outlining strategies for fostering greater collaboration.

The Importance of Civil Society and Community Participation

Civil society organizations (CSOs) and local communities often possess invaluable local knowledge, cultural insights, and grassroots networks that are critical for developing context-specific solutions to plastic pollution. By engaging with communities and empowering local stakeholders, partnerships can harness collective expertise and mobilize resources for more sustainable outcomes.

Building Trust and Empowering Communities

Successful partnerships are built on trust, mutual respect, and shared goals. When collaborating with civil society and local communities, it is essential to prioritize inclusivity, transparency, and meaningful engagement. Empowering communities to take ownership of plastic pollution mitigation initiatives fosters a sense of stewardship and promotes long-term sustainability.

Examples of Civil Society-Led Initiatives

1. Community-Led Cleanup Campaigns:

CSOs often organize beach cleanups, river cleanups, and neighbourhood cleanup events to raise awareness about plastic pollution and mobilize community action. These initiatives not only remove plastic waste from the environment but also foster a sense of pride and responsibility among participants.

2. Education and Awareness Programs:

CSOs play a crucial role in delivering educational workshops, school programs, and public outreach campaigns to educate communities about the impacts of plastic pollution and promote behaviour change. By empowering individuals with knowledge and skills, these initiatives empower communities to take proactive steps towards reducing plastic waste.

3. Plastic-Free Initiatives:

CSOs collaborate with local businesses, schools, and government agencies to promote plastic-free alternatives, such as reusable bags, water bottles, and straws. These initiatives encourage the adoption of sustainable practices and help reduce the demand for single-use plastics in local communities.

Strategies for Effective Collaboration

1. Participatory Decision-Making:

Involve community members in all stages of project planning, implementation, and evaluation to ensure that initiatives are responsive to local needs and priorities.

2. Capacity Building:

Provide training and capacity-building opportunities to empower community leaders, youth groups, and other stakeholders to take active roles in plastic pollution mitigation efforts.

3. Networking and Knowledge Sharing:

Facilitate collaboration and knowledge exchange among CSOs, community groups, government agencies, and other stakeholders to leverage collective expertise and resources.

4. Advocacy and Policy Engagement:

Mobilize civil society networks to advocate for stronger regulations, policies, and incentives to address plastic pollution at local, national, and regional levels.

Case Study: The Caribbean Youth Environment Network (CYEN)

CYEN is a regional network of youth-led environmental organizations across the Caribbean, dedicated to promoting sustainable development and environmental conservation. Through grassroots initiatives, advocacy campaigns, and educational programs, CYEN engages young people in efforts to address plastic pollution and build resilient communities.

Partnerships and collaborations between civil society organizations, local communities, and other stakeholders are thus vital for mitigating plastic pollution in Small Island Developing States. By harnessing the collective wisdom, energy, and resources of diverse stakeholders, these partnerships can drive positive change and create a more sustainable future for SIDS and the planet.

Partnerships and collaborations among governmental and non-governmental organizations, the private sector, and civil society are indispensable in the fight against plastic pollution in Small Island Developing States. By working together towards shared goals, leveraging complementary strengths, and fostering inclusive and participatory approaches, these partnerships have the potential to catalyse transformative change and create a more sustainable future for SIDS and the global community.

In this chapter, I highlighted the importance of partnerships and collaborations across governmental and non-governmental organizations, the private sector, and civil society in addressing plastic pollution in Small Island Developing States (SIDS). These partnerships are essential for mobilizing resources, sharing expertise, and implementing effective solutions at local, national, and international levels.

Chapter - 10
Future Perspectives

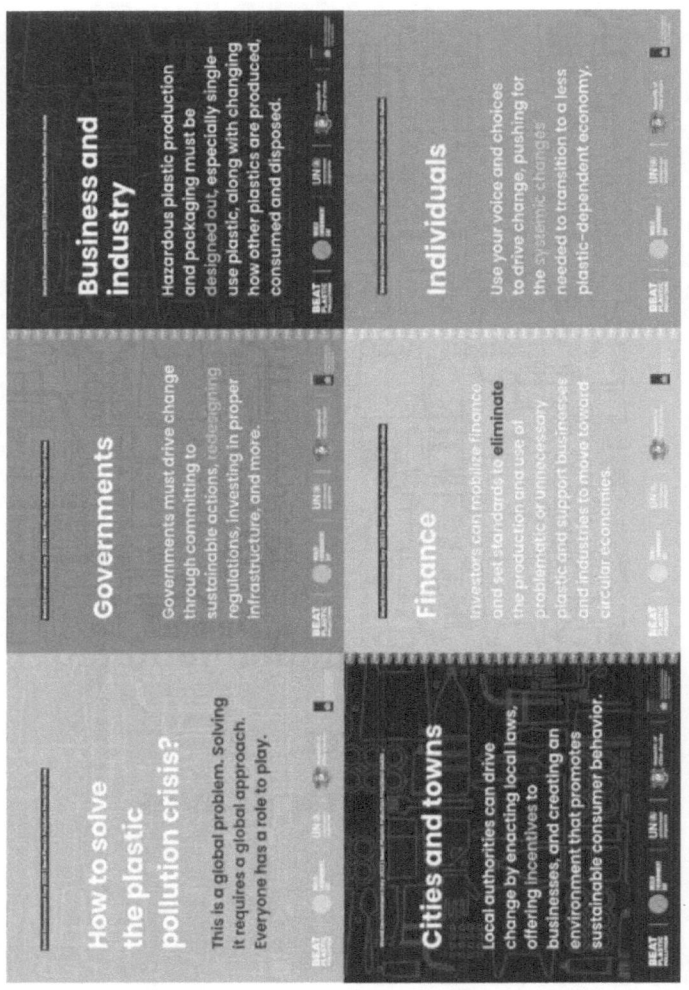

Future Perspectives

As we look to the future, optimism must be tempered with realism. This chapter considers emerging trends and technologies, outlines long-term strategies for SIDS, and underscores the importance of sustained commitment to the fight against plastic pollution.

As we stand at the cusp of a new era in the fight against plastic pollution, it is imperative to look ahead with both optimism and pragmatism. The future holds promise for innovative solutions, strengthened partnerships, and concerted global action. In this chapter, we explore emerging trends and technologies, outline long-term strategies for Small Island Developing States (SIDS), and consider the broader context of the global fight against plastic pollution.

Emerging Trends and Technologies

The rapid pace of technological advancement offers unprecedented opportunities for tackling plastic pollution in SIDS. From advanced recycling technologies to novel materials and innovative waste management systems, a plethora of solutions are on the horizon.

As we look ahead to the future of mitigating plastic pollution in Small Island Developing States (SIDS), it is essential to explore emerging trends and technologies that offer promising solutions to this complex challenge. This chapter examines innovative approaches that harness the power of science, technology, and collaboration to address plastic pollution in SIDS and pave the way for a more sustainable future.

1. Advanced Waste Management Systems

Emerging trends in waste management emphasize the importance of adopting integrated and decentralized systems tailored to the unique needs of SIDS. Advanced waste sorting and recycling technologies, such as optical sorting and chemical recycling, hold the potential to improve the efficiency and effectiveness of waste management processes. Additionally, the use of mobile recycling units and community-based recycling initiatives can help increase recycling rates and reduce the reliance on landfilling and incineration.

2. Biodegradable and Compostable Plastics

The development of biodegradable and compostable plastics presents a promising alternative to traditional petroleum-based plastics. These materials are designed to break down more readily in natural environments, reducing the long-term accumulation of plastic waste. However, careful consideration must be given to ensure that biodegradable plastics are compatible with existing waste management infrastructure and do not contribute to contamination or unintended environmental impacts.

3. Blockchain Technology for Supply Chain Transparency

Blockchain technology offers a novel approach to enhancing transparency and traceability throughout the plastic supply chain. By recording transactions and movements of plastic materials on a decentralized ledger, blockchain can help verify the origins of plastics, track their journey from production to disposal, and hold stakeholders accountable for their environmental footprint. Implementing blockchain-based solutions can empower consumers, businesses, and regulators to make more informed decisions and incentivize sustainable practices.

4. Artificial Intelligence and Machine Learning for Monitoring and Detection

Advances in artificial intelligence (AI) and machine learning have the potential to revolutionize the monitoring and detection of plastic pollution in marine environments. AI-powered algorithms can analyse satellite imagery, underwater drones, and sensor data to identify plastic hotspots, track plastic debris movement, and predict potential accumulation areas. By leveraging AI and machine learning technologies, SIDS can enhance their capacity for early detection and rapid response to plastic pollution incidents.

5. Eco-Friendly Packaging Innovations

Innovations in eco-friendly packaging materials offer opportunities to reduce the environmental impact of single-use plastics in SIDS. From biodegradable packaging made from plant-based materials to edible packaging that dissolves in water, these alternatives prioritize sustainability and circularity. Additionally, initiatives such as refillable and reusable packaging systems promote waste reduction and encourage a shift towards more sustainable consumption patterns among consumers and businesses.

6. Ocean Cleanup Technologies

Ocean cleanup technologies continue to evolve, offering new tools and methods for removing plastic pollution from marine environments. From passive floating barriers that capture plastic debris to autonomous cleanup vessels equipped with collection systems, these technologies demonstrate the potential to scale up cleanup efforts and mitigate the impact of plastic pollution on marine ecosystems. Collaborative initiatives such as The Ocean Cleanup project exemplify the power of innovation and engineering in addressing the global challenge of ocean plastic pollution.

7. Data-driven Decision-making and Policy Innovation

Data-driven approaches are increasingly shaping decision-making and policy innovation in the fight against plastic pollution. By leveraging data analytics, modelling, and predictive tools, policymakers can identify priority areas for intervention, evaluate the effectiveness of mitigation strategies, and allocate resources more efficiently. Furthermore, the development of adaptive governance frameworks that integrate scientific evidence, stakeholder input, and real-time monitoring can facilitate more agile and responsive policy responses to plastic pollution in SIDS.

8. Public-private Partnerships and Collaborative Initiatives

Public-private partnerships and collaborative initiatives play a vital role in driving innovation and scaling up solutions to plastic pollution in SIDS. By bringing together governments, businesses, academia, and civil society organizations, these partnerships leverage diverse expertise, resources, and networks to catalyse positive change. From industry-led initiatives to research consortia and multi-stakeholder platforms, collaborative efforts foster innovation, knowledge-sharing, and collective action towards a plastic-free future for SIDS.

Emerging trends and technologies offer unprecedented opportunities to address plastic pollution in Small Island Developing States and chart a course towards a more sustainable and resilient future. By embracing innovation, collaboration, and forward-thinking approaches, SIDS can lead the way in turning the tide on plastic pollution and safeguarding the health of our oceans for generations to come.

Long-term Strategies for SIDS

Addressing plastic pollution in Small Island Developing States (SIDS) requires a comprehensive and sustained approach that goes beyond short-term fixes. This chapter explores the development and implementation of long-term strategies aimed at mitigating plastic pollution in SIDS, focusing on proactive measures to prevent plastic waste generation, enhance waste management systems, and foster a culture of sustainability.

1. Prevention through Policy and Regulation

➤ Phasing Out Single-Use Plastics:

Implementing bans or restrictions on single-use plastics such as plastic bags, straws, and Styrofoam containers can significantly reduce plastic waste generation at the source.

➤ Extended Producer Responsibility (EPR):

Establishing EPR policies that hold producers accountable for the entire lifecycle of their products, including collection, recycling, and proper disposal, incentivizes the design of more sustainable packaging and products.

➤ Promoting Sustainable Consumption:

Encouraging consumers to make environmentally conscious choices through awareness campaigns, eco-labelling, and incentives for reusable alternatives can help shift societal norms towards sustainability.

2. Strengthening Waste Management Infrastructure

➤ **Investing in Collection and Recycling Facilities:**

Expanding access to waste collection services and investing in recycling infrastructure, including material recovery facilities and community recycling centres, can improve the management of plastic waste.

➤ **Promoting Circular Economy Principles:**

Embracing the principles of a circular economy, where resources are reused, recycled, and repurposed, can minimize the environmental impact of plastic production and consumption.

➤ **Innovative Waste-to-Energy Solutions:**

Exploring innovative technologies such as waste-to-energy systems and biogas generation can help reduce the volume of plastic waste sent to landfills while also providing renewable energy sources.

3. Education and Awareness Campaigns

➢ **Environmental Education in Schools:**
Integrating environmental education into school curricula fosters awareness and empowers future generations to become stewards of their environment.

➢ **Community Engagement Programs:**
Engaging local communities through outreach programs, workshops, and cleanup initiatives cultivates a sense of ownership and collective responsibility for waste management and pollution prevention.

➢ **Media and Communication Campaigns:**
Leveraging traditional and digital media platforms to raise awareness about the impacts of plastic pollution and promote sustainable behaviours can drive societal change.

4. Harnessing Technology and Innovation

➤ Data-driven Decision-making:

Utilizing data analytics, remote sensing technologies, and geographic information systems (GIS) can inform evidence-based policy decisions and prioritize areas for intervention.

➤ Blockchain for Supply Chain Transparency:

Implementing blockchain technology to track and trace the lifecycle of plastic products enhances supply chain transparency and accountability, facilitating responsible production and consumption practices.

➤ Emerging Cleanup Technologies:

Investing in research and development of innovative cleanup technologies, such as autonomous drones and ocean-cleaning vessels, can complement waste management efforts and remove plastic debris from marine environments.

5. Integrating Plastic Pollution Mitigation into Sustainable Development Goals

➤ Aligning with International Agendas:

Integrating plastic pollution mitigation goals into national development plans and aligning with international frameworks such as the United Nations Sustainable Development Goals (SDGs) ensures a holistic approach to sustainable development.

➤ Cross-sectoral Collaboration:

Fostering collaboration among government agencies, civil society organizations, private sector stakeholders, and academia facilitates synergies and maximizes the impact of interventions across sectors.

6. Long-term Monitoring and Evaluation

➤ Establishing Baseline Data:

Conducting comprehensive assessments of plastic pollution levels, waste generation rates, and marine debris hotspots establishes baseline data for monitoring progress and evaluating the effectiveness of interventions.

➤ Regular Reporting Mechanisms:

Implementing robust monitoring and reporting mechanisms enables continuous tracking of progress towards plastic pollution mitigation targets and facilitates adaptive management approaches.

Mitigating plastic pollution in SIDS requires a multifaceted approach that addresses both the symptoms and root causes of the problem. Long-term strategies must be grounded in sustainability, resilience, and inclusivity, taking into account the unique socio-economic and environmental contexts of SIDS.

➤ Integrated Waste Management Systems:

Developing robust waste management infrastructure is essential for reducing the influx of plastic waste into the environment. SIDS can invest in comprehensive waste collection, sorting, recycling, and disposal facilities, prioritizing the adoption of decentralized and community-based approaches.

➤ Circular Economy Principles:

Embracing the principles of the circular economy can help SIDS transition towards more sustainable consumption and production patterns. By designing out waste, promoting reuse and recycling, and prioritizing resource efficiency, SIDS can minimize their reliance on single-use plastics and create closed-loop systems that regenerate natural capital.

➤ Eco-friendly Policies and Incentives:

Governments and policymakers in SIDS can enact legislation and regulations that incentivize sustainable practices and discourage the use of environmentally harmful materials. Measures such as plastic bans, extended producer responsibility schemes, and green procurement policies can drive behavioural change and promote a culture of sustainability.

> **Community Engagement and Education:**

Empowering communities through education, awareness-raising, and capacity-building initiatives is critical for fostering a sense of ownership and responsibility towards plastic pollution mitigation. SIDS can leverage traditional knowledge, cultural values, and indigenous practices to instil a deep-rooted ethos of environmental stewardship and conservation.

Long-term strategies for mitigating plastic pollution in Small Island Developing States require a multi-faceted approach that addresses the root causes of plastic waste generation, strengthens waste management infrastructure, fosters community engagement, harnesses technology and innovation, and integrates plastic pollution mitigation into broader sustainable development agendas. By adopting proactive measures and working collaboratively across sectors and stakeholders, SIDS can pave the way towards a cleaner, healthier, and more resilient future for their communities and their marine environments.

The Global Fight Against Plastic Pollution

While SIDS face unique challenges in tackling plastic pollution, they are not alone in their struggle. The global community must unite in solidarity to address this shared threat to the health of our planet and its inhabitants.

Plastic pollution knows no boundaries. It transcends national borders, affecting communities and ecosystems worldwide. In this chapter, we examine the collective efforts of the international community to combat plastic pollution and the implications for Small Island Developing States (SIDS). By understanding the global context and initiatives, we can better identify opportunities for collaboration and leverage resources to mitigate plastic pollution in SIDS.

The Scale of the Problem

Plastic pollution has reached crisis proportions, with an estimated 8 million metric tons of plastic entering the ocean every year. This global issue poses significant threats to marine life, human health, and coastal economies. Plastic debris can travel vast distances, circulating through ocean currents and accumulating in remote areas, including SIDS. The interconnected nature of the ocean means that no country is immune to the impacts of plastic pollution.

International Agreements and Initiatives

Recognizing the urgency of the problem, the international community has taken steps to address plastic pollution through various agreements and initiatives:

1. United Nations Environment Programme (UNEP):

UNEP leads global efforts to combat marine litter and microplastics through initiatives such as the

Global Partnership on Marine Litter and the Clean Seas Campaign. These efforts raise awareness, promote policy action, and support capacity-building in countries, including SIDS.

2. Basel Convention on the Control of Transboundary Movements of Hazardous Wastes and Their Disposal:

The Basel Convention, amended in 2019 to include plastic waste, aims to regulate the transboundary movement of plastic waste and promote environmentally sound management. This is particularly relevant for SIDS, which may receive plastic waste from international sources.

3. The Ocean Cleanup:

Innovative projects such as The Ocean Cleanup aim to remove plastic debris from the ocean using advanced technologies. While these initiatives primarily focus on high-impact areas such as ocean gyres, they contribute to global efforts to reduce the overall burden of plastic pollution.

Corporate Responsibility and Industry Initiatives

Beyond governmental action, corporations and industries play a crucial role in addressing plastic pollution:

1. Plastic Industry Initiatives:

Some companies within the plastic industry have launched initiatives to improve recycling infrastructure, develop sustainable packaging alternatives, and reduce plastic waste. Collaboration between industry stakeholders and governments is essential to drive meaningful change.

2. Extended Producer Responsibility (EPR):

EPR programs hold producers accountable for the end-of-life management of their products, encouraging them to design for recyclability and invest in waste management systems. Implementing EPR policies can help reduce the flow of plastic waste into the environment, benefiting SIDS and other regions.

Civil Society and Grassroots Movements

Civil society organizations and grassroots movements play a vital role in raising awareness, mobilizing communities, and advocating for policy change:

1. Plastic Pollution Coalitions:

Organizations such as the Plastic Pollution Coalition unite individuals, businesses, and NGOs in a global movement to reduce plastic pollution. Through campaigns, education, and advocacy, these coalitions amplify the voices of affected communities, including those in SIDS.

2. Community-Led Initiatives:

Local communities in SIDS are taking action to address plastic pollution through beach cleanups, recycling programs, and sustainable alternatives. These grassroots efforts empower communities to be agents of change and foster a sense of ownership over environmental stewardship.

Challenges and Opportunities for SIDS

While global efforts to combat plastic pollution are commendable, SIDS face unique challenges and opportunities in this endeavour:

1. Limited Resources:

SIDS often have limited financial and technical resources to implement comprehensive waste management systems and address plastic pollution effectively. International support and cooperation are critical to bridge these gaps and build resilience in SIDS communities.

2. Ecosystem Vulnerability:

The fragile ecosystems of SIDS are particularly vulnerable to the impacts of plastic pollution, threatening biodiversity, fisheries, and tourism. Integrated approaches that consider the socio-economic context and cultural values of SIDS are essential for sustainable solutions.

3. Opportunities for Innovation:

Despite these challenges, SIDS are hubs of innovation, creativity, and resilience. By harnessing traditional knowledge, leveraging new technologies, and fostering partnerships, SIDS can pioneer innovative solutions to mitigate plastic pollution and lead by example on the global stage.

➤ **International Cooperation and Collaboration:**

Strengthening international cooperation and collaboration is essential for coordinating efforts, sharing best practices, and mobilizing resources to combat plastic pollution. Initiatives such as the UN Decade of Ocean Science for Sustainable Development and the Global Plastics Treaty offer platforms for collective action and dialogue among nations.

➤ **Corporate Responsibility and Accountability:**

The private sector has a crucial role to play in driving innovation, scaling up solutions, and reducing the environmental footprint of plastic production and consumption. Businesses can adopt sustainable business practices, invest in research and development of eco-friendly technologies, and embrace product stewardship principles to minimize plastic pollution.

➤ Civil Society Mobilization:

Civil society organizations, grassroots movements, and non-governmental actors play a vital role in raising awareness, advocating for policy change, and holding governments and corporations accountable for their actions. By mobilizing public support and driving bottom-up initiatives, civil society can catalyse transformative change and amplify the voices of affected communities.

The global fight against plastic pollution is a collective endeavour that requires collaboration, innovation, and sustained commitment from all stakeholders. While SIDS face unique challenges in addressing plastic pollution, they also possess untapped potential for leadership and innovation. By joining forces with the international community, SIDS can turn the tide on plastic pollution and pave the way towards a more sustainable future for all.

In conclusion, the future of plastic pollution mitigation in Small Island Developing States is characterized by both challenges and opportunities. By embracing innovation, fostering collaboration, and committing to long-term sustainability, SIDS can pave the way towards a cleaner, healthier, and more resilient future for generations to come. The journey ahead will be arduous, but with determination, creativity, and collective action, we can turn the tide in the fight against plastic pollution.

In this chapter, we gazed into the crystal ball of the future, envisioning a world where plastic pollution is no longer a looming threat but a distant memory. Through innovation, collaboration, and sustained effort, we can chart a course towards a more sustainable and resilient future for Small Island Developing States and the planet as a whole.

Chapter - 11
Conclusion

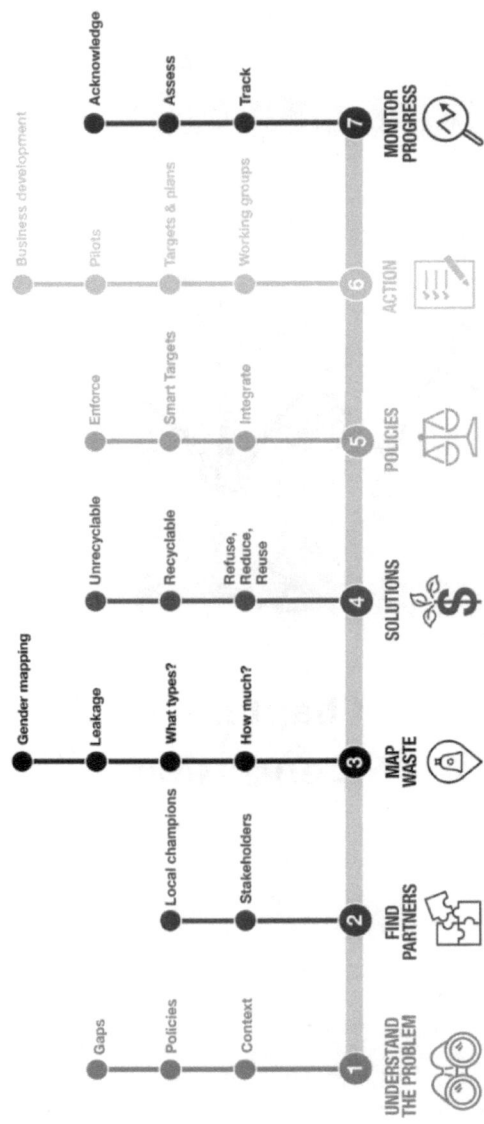

Conclusion

In closing, this book emphasizes the urgency of action in mitigating plastic pollution in SIDS. It calls for a renewed sense of purpose, solidarity, and determination in confronting this shared challenge and offers hope for a more sustainable and resilient future.

As we reach the culmination of our exploration into mitigating plastic pollution in Small Island Developing States (SIDS), it is imperative to reflect on the urgency of action and the hope for a sustainable future. Throughout this journey, we have witnessed the profound impacts of plastic pollution on the environment, economies, and communities of SIDS. From the shores of the Caribbean to the islands of the Pacific, the scourge of plastic waste threatens to undermine the very fabric of life in these vulnerable nations.

The Urgency of Action

Plastic pollution poses an existential threat to Small Island Developing States (SIDS), demanding urgent and concerted action at local, regional, and global levels. This chapter explores the pressing need for decisive measures to address the crisis, highlighting the immediate risks and long-term consequences of inaction.

The Current State of Affairs

Plastic pollution has reached alarming levels in SIDS, with these vulnerable nations bearing a disproportionate burden of its impacts. Despite their small size and limited resources, SIDS are on the front lines of this global crisis, contending with mounting piles of plastic waste, degraded marine ecosystems, and threats to public health and livelihoods.

Environmental Degradation

The pervasive presence of plastic pollution in SIDS has dire consequences for fragile marine ecosystems, pristine beaches, and iconic wildlife. Coral reefs, vital for biodiversity and coastal protection, are smothered by plastic debris, while seabirds, turtles, and marine mammals suffer from entanglement and ingestion of plastic waste. The loss of biodiversity not only undermines ecological resilience but also threatens the cultural identity and traditional practices of SIDS communities closely linked to the sea.

Economic Implications

Plastic pollution exacts a heavy toll on the economies of SIDS, undermining key sectors such as tourism, fisheries, and agriculture. Beaches strewn with plastic debris repel tourists, depriving SIDS of vital revenue and employment opportunities. Fishing grounds contaminated with plastic waste endanger seafood supplies and jeopardize the livelihoods of coastal communities dependent on marine resources for sustenance and income. Moreover, the costs of cleaning up plastic pollution and mitigating its impacts further strain already stretched budgets, diverting funds from essential services and development priorities.

Public Health Risks

The proliferation of plastic pollution in SIDS poses significant risks to public health, with potentially grave consequences for human well-being and quality of life. Plastic debris leaches toxic chemicals into the marine environment, contaminating seafood and entering the food chain, ultimately exposing humans to harmful substances. Moreover, the improper disposal of plastic waste contributes to the proliferation of disease vectors, such as mosquitoes breeding in stagnant water trapped in discarded plastic containers, increasing the incidence of vector-borne illnesses like dengue fever and malaria.

Climate Change Amplification

Plastic pollution exacerbates the impacts of climate change in SIDS, compounding existing vulnerabilities and threatening sustainable development efforts. The production, transportation, and disposal of plastic contribute to greenhouse gas emissions and energy consumption, further accelerating global warming and sea-level rise. In a cruel irony, SIDS, which contribute minimally to climate change, bear the brunt of its consequences, facing increased frequency and intensity of extreme weather events, coastal erosion, and inundation.

The Imperative for Action

The urgency of action to address plastic pollution in SIDS cannot be overstated. Time is of the essence as the window of opportunity to prevent irreversible harm to ecosystems, economies, and societies rapidly narrows. Delaying action only amplifies the magnitude and complexity of the problem, prolonging the suffering of present and future generations.

A Call to Arms

The challenge of mitigating plastic pollution in SIDS requires a comprehensive, multi-faceted approach that addresses the root causes, strengthens resilience, and fosters collaboration across sectors and stakeholders. Governments, civil society, the private sector, and international organizations must mobilize resources, share knowledge, and coordinate efforts to tackle this shared challenge.

Empowering Communities

Central to the success of any action against plastic pollution is the empowerment of local communities in SIDS. Engaging communities in sustainable waste management practices, promoting environmental education and awareness, and supporting grassroots initiatives are essential steps in building resilience and fostering a sense of ownership and stewardship over natural resources.

Advocating for Change

Effective advocacy and policy reform are critical in driving systemic change and shaping a conducive regulatory environment for plastic pollution mitigation in SIDS. Governments must enact and enforce legislation to restrict the production and consumption of single-use plastics, promote eco-friendly alternatives, and invest in infrastructure for waste collection, recycling, and disposal.

International Solidarity

The global nature of plastic pollution necessitates international cooperation and solidarity in addressing its root causes and mitigating its impacts. Developed countries must provide financial and technical assistance to SIDS, recognizing their historical responsibility and capacity constraints. Multilateral agreements, such as the Basel Convention on the Control of Transboundary Movements of Hazardous Wastes, offer frameworks for collaboration and capacity-building in waste management and pollution prevention.

In conclusion, the urgency of action to mitigate plastic pollution in Small Island Developing States cannot be overstated. The time to act is now, before irreversible harm is inflicted upon the fragile ecosystems, economies, and societies of these vulnerable nations. By embracing the imperative for action, fostering collaboration, and empowering communities, we can turn the tide on plastic pollution and chart a course towards a more sustainable and resilient future for all.

Hope for a Sustainable Future

Amidst the urgency of action, there is also reason for hope. Across SIDS, communities are rising to the challenge, embracing innovative solutions, and forging partnerships to tackle plastic pollution head-on. From grassroots initiatives led by local activists to regional collaborations facilitated by international organizations, there is a growing momentum for change.

In the battle against plastic pollution in Small Island Developing States (SIDS), hope emerges as a powerful force driving innovation, resilience, and collective action. Despite the daunting challenges posed by plastic waste, there are reasons to be optimistic about the prospects for a sustainable future. This chapter explores the sources of hope and the pathways towards lasting solutions in the fight against plastic pollution in SIDS.

1. Community Engagement and Empowerment

- One source of hope lies in the growing momentum of grassroots movements and community-led initiatives aimed at tackling plastic pollution at the local level. From beach cleanups and recycling drives to education and awareness campaigns, communities in SIDS are taking ownership of the issue and driving positive change.

- By empowering local stakeholders, including indigenous communities and youth groups, to become active participants in plastic pollution mitigation efforts, SIDS can tap into a wealth of knowledge, creativity, and cultural wisdom. This bottom-up approach fosters a sense of ownership and responsibility, ensuring that solutions are tailored to the unique needs and circumstances of each island community.

2. Innovation and Technology

- The rapid pace of technological innovation offers promising opportunities for addressing plastic pollution in SIDS. Advances in waste management technologies, such as mobile recycling units and community-based composting systems, enable decentralized approaches to waste management, reducing reliance on centralized infrastructure.

- Emerging technologies, such as biodegradable plastics, enzymatic recycling, and blockchain-based tracking systems, hold the potential to revolutionize the way we produce, consume, and manage plastics. By investing in research and development, SIDS can harness the power of innovation to create more sustainable alternatives and close the loop on plastic waste.

3. Policy and Governance

- Effective governance and policy frameworks are essential for driving systemic change and scaling up plastic pollution mitigation efforts in SIDS. By enacting legislation to ban single-use plastics, implement extended producer responsibility schemes, and promote circular economy principles, governments can create an enabling environment for sustainable practices to thrive.

- Regional collaboration and knowledge sharing play a crucial role in strengthening policy coherence and fostering collective action on plastic pollution. Through platforms such as the Caribbean Community (CARICOM) and the Pacific Islands Forum (PIF), SIDS can leverage their collective voice and influence to advocate for stronger environmental protection measures at the regional and international levels.

4. Education and Awareness

- Education is a powerful tool for instilling values of environmental stewardship and fostering a culture of sustainability from an early age. By integrating environmental education into school curricula, promoting eco-friendly practices in communities, and leveraging digital media platforms for outreach, SIDS can cultivate a new generation of environmentally conscious citizens.

- Public awareness campaigns, art exhibitions, and storytelling initiatives are effective ways to engage the wider public and mobilize support for plastic pollution mitigation efforts. By leveraging the power of storytelling and visual communication, SIDS can inspire action, foster empathy, and build solidarity across diverse stakeholders.

5. Partnerships and Collaboration

- Collaboration is key to overcoming the complex and interconnected challenges of plastic pollution in SIDS. By forging partnerships with governments, civil society organizations, academia, and the private sector, SIDS can pool resources, share expertise, and amplify their impact on a global scale.

- Multilateral initiatives, such as the Clean Seas campaign led by the United Nations Environment Programme (UNEP) and the Global Plastic Action Partnership (GPAP) convened by the World Economic Forum, provide platforms for collaborative action and knowledge exchange. By actively participating in these initiatives, SIDS can strengthen their capacity for collective action and drive progress towards a plastic-free future.

Thus, while the challenges of plastic pollution in Small Island Developing States are formidable, there are reasons to be hopeful about the prospects for a sustainable future. By embracing innovation, fostering community engagement, strengthening governance frameworks, promoting education and awareness, and forging partnerships for collective action, SIDS can chart a course towards a cleaner, healthier, and more resilient future for generations to come.

The transition to a sustainable future will not be easy, but it is within our reach. By harnessing the power of innovation, technology, and collective action, we can turn the tide on plastic pollution and chart a course towards a healthier, cleaner, and more resilient planet. The challenges we face are daunting, but they are not insurmountable.

In the words of Margaret Mead, "Never doubt that a small group of thoughtful, committed citizens can change the world; indeed, it's the only thing that ever has." As we look to the future, let us draw inspiration from the countless individuals, organizations, and communities who are leading the charge against plastic pollution. Together, we can make a difference.

Tides of Change: Mitigating Plastic Pollution in Small Island Developing States is more than just a book—it is a call to action, a rallying cry for all those who believe in the power of collective action to effect positive change. As we embark on this journey towards a plastic-free future, let us do so with a sense of purpose, determination, and hope.

The tides of change are upon us. Let us seize this moment and build a brighter, more sustainable future for generations to come.

In the conclusion, I aimed to emphasize the urgency of action in addressing plastic pollution in SIDS while also instilling hope for a sustainable future. I highlighted the importance of collective action, innovation, and partnerships in overcoming the challenges we face and charting a course towards a cleaner, healthier planet.

Epilogue
A Call to Action

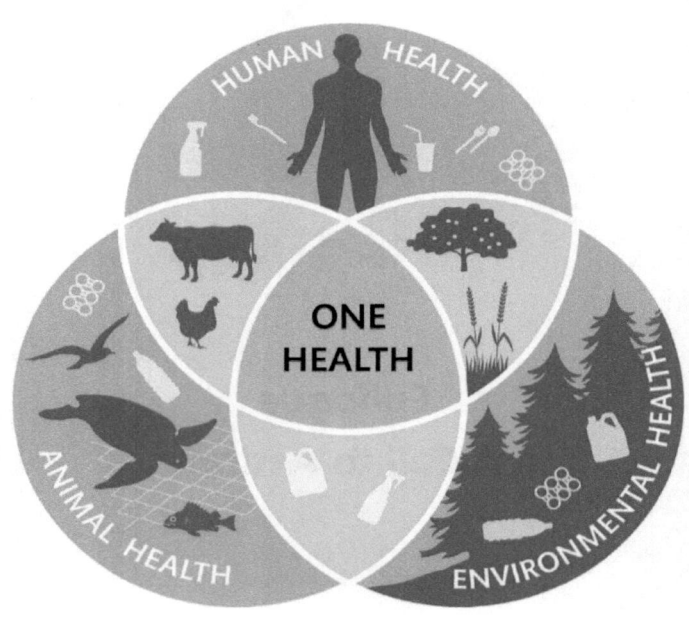

A Call to Action

As we come to the end of our exploration into mitigating plastic pollution in Small Island Developing States (SIDS), we are reminded that this journey is far from over. The challenges we face are complex and multifaceted, but so too are the opportunities for meaningful change and progress.

Throughout this book, we have delved into the myriad ways in which plastic pollution impacts the environment, economy, and societies of SIDS. We have examined the root causes of this crisis, from consumer behaviour to inadequate waste management systems, and explored the innovative solutions and technologies that offer hope for a brighter future.

Yet, amidst the urgency of action, there is also cause for optimism. Across SIDS and beyond, individuals, communities, governments, and organizations are coming together to confront the scourge of plastic pollution head-on. From grassroots initiatives to international collaborations, the collective efforts of stakeholders at all levels are driving positive change and fostering a sense of shared responsibility for our planet.

But there is still much work to be done. As we look ahead, we must remain vigilant in our efforts to reduce plastic consumption, improve waste management infrastructure, and promote sustainable alternatives to single-use plastics. We must continue to advocate for stronger policies and regulations, while also supporting those on the frontlines of the fight against plastic pollution.

Moreover, we must recognize that the battle against plastic pollution is not just about protecting the environment—it is also about safeguarding the livelihoods and well-being of SIDS communities, who are on the frontline of this crisis. By addressing the root causes of plastic pollution and building resilience in the face of environmental challenges, we can create a more sustainable and equitable future for all.

In closing, let us remember that we are all stewards of our planet, entrusted with the task of preserving it for future generations. The tides of change are upon us, and it is up to each and every one of us to rise to the challenge and chart a course towards a cleaner, healthier, and more sustainable world.

Together, we can turn the tide on plastic pollution and ensure that the oceans–and the SIDS communities that depend on them–thrive for generations to come.

The journey begins with each step we take, each choice we make, and each commitment we honour. Let us embark on this journey together, united in our determination to make a difference.

The tides of change are calling—are you ready to answer?

In this epilogue, I aimed to encapsulate the essence of the book's message and inspire readers to take action in the fight against plastic pollution in SIDS. Let me know if you'd like any adjustments or further elaboration!

Dr. Chirag Bhimani

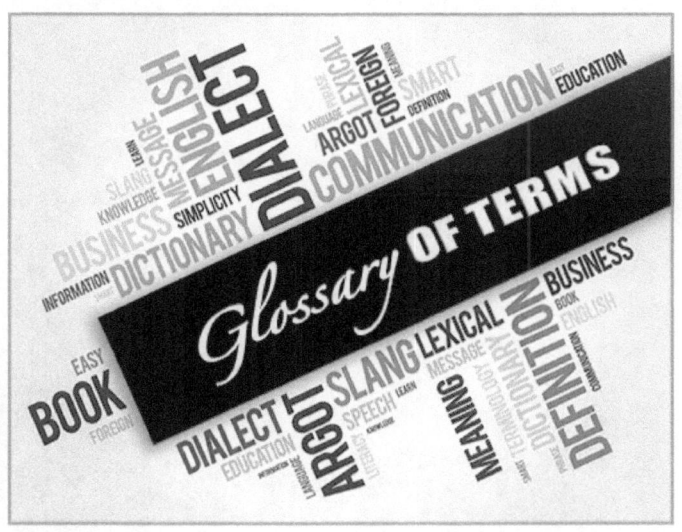

Glossary of Terms

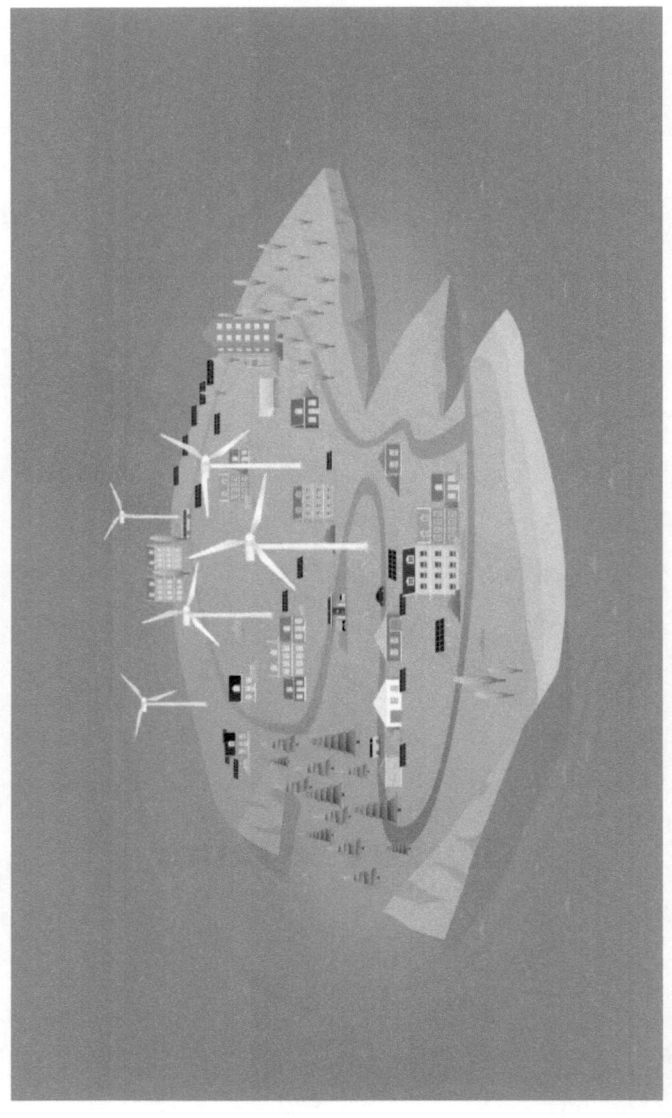

In the fight against plastic pollution in Small Island Developing States (SIDS), understanding key terminology is essential for effective communication and collaboration. This glossary provides definitions and explanations of terms commonly used in discussions surrounding plastic pollution mitigation efforts in SIDS.

1. Plastic Pollution: The presence of plastic waste in the environment, particularly in oceans and waterways, causing harm to marine life, ecosystems, and human health.

2. Single-Use Plastics: Disposable plastic items designed for one-time use before being discarded, including items such as plastic bags, straws, and food packaging.

3. Microplastics: Tiny plastic particles measuring less than 5 millimetres in size, often resulting from the breakdown of larger plastic items or manufactured as microbeads in personal care products.

4. Marine Debris: Any persistent solid material that is manufactured or processed and directly or indirectly, intentionally or unintentionally, disposed of or abandoned into the marine environment or the Great Lakes.

5. Waste Management: The collection, transportation, processing, recycling, and disposal of waste materials, including plastics, in a manner that minimizes environmental impact and maximizes resource recovery.

6. Circular Economy: An economic system aimed at minimizing waste and maximizing the use of resources by keeping materials in circulation for as long as possible through recycling, reusing, and reducing consumption.

7. Biodiversity: The variety of life forms, including species diversity, genetic diversity, and ecosystem diversity, within a given ecosystem, region, or the entire planet.

8. Ecosystem Services: The benefits that humans derive from ecosystems, including provisioning services (such as food and water), regulating services (such as climate regulation and waste decomposition), supporting services (such as nutrient cycling), and cultural services (such as recreational and aesthetic value).

9. Pollution Prevention: The practice of reducing or eliminating pollution at its source through changes in production, consumption, or waste management practices, rather than treating or cleaning up pollution after it has been generated.

10. Sustainable Development Goals (SDGs): A set of 17 global goals adopted by the United Nations General Assembly in 2015, aimed at addressing social, economic, and environmental challenges to achieve a more sustainable future by 2030.

11. Adaptation: The process of adjusting to changes in environmental conditions, such as climate change, in order to reduce vulnerability and increase resilience.

12. Mitigation: Actions taken to reduce or prevent the emission of greenhouse gases or other pollutants in order to lessen the severity of climate change or other environmental impacts.

13. Stakeholder Engagement: The process of involving individuals, communities, organizations, and other stakeholders in decision-making processes related to environmental management and policy development.

14. Community-Based Conservation: Conservation efforts that involve local communities in the planning, implementation, and management of environmental projects, recognizing their role as stewards of natural resources.

15. Biodegradable: Capable of being broken down by natural biological processes, such as bacteria or fungi, into simpler substances that can be absorbed by the environment without causing harm.

16. Ocean Acidification: The ongoing decrease in the pH of the Earth's oceans, primarily caused by the absorption of carbon dioxide from the atmosphere, which can have harmful effects on marine life, particularly organisms with calcium carbonate shells or skeletons.

17. Sustainable Tourism: Tourism that seeks to minimize its negative impacts on the environment, culture, and communities while maximizing the benefits to local economies and ecosystems.

18. Invasive Species: Non-native species that have been introduced into a new ecosystem and have the potential to cause harm to native species, disrupt ecosystems, and threaten biodiversity.

19. Eco-Tourism: Responsible travel to natural areas that conserves the environment, sustains the well-being of local communities, and involves interpretation and education.

20. Blue Economy: An economic model that seeks to promote sustainable development and conservation of ocean resources while generating economic growth and improving livelihoods.

Understanding these terms is essential for developing effective strategies and implementing successful initiatives to mitigate plastic pollution in Small Island Developing States. By working together and leveraging the collective knowledge and expertise of stakeholders, we can address this urgent environmental challenge and create a more sustainable future for SIDS and the planet as a whole.

References

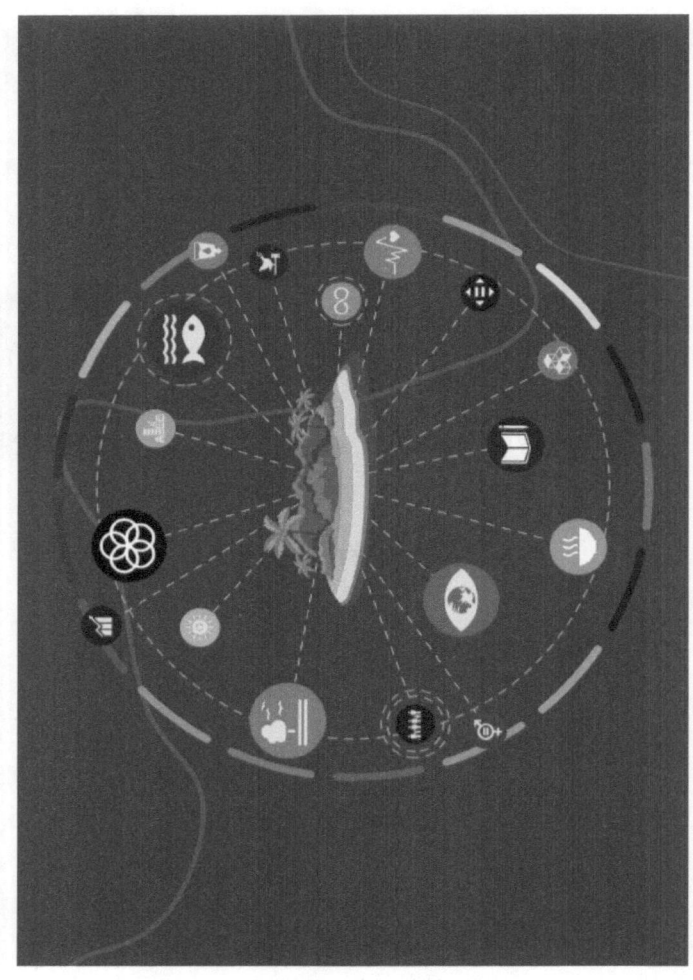

1. Barnes, D. K. A., Galgani, F., Thompson, R. C., & Barlaz, M. (2009). Accumulation and fragmentation of plastic debris in global environments. Philosophical Transactions of the Royal Society B: Biological Sciences, 364(1526), 1985–1998. [DOI: 10.1098/rstb.2008.0205] (https://doi.org/10.1098/rstb.2008.0205)

2. United Nations Environment Programme (UNEP). (2016). Marine Plastic Debris and Microplastics: Global lessons and research to inspire action and guide policy change. Nairobi, Kenya: UNEP. [UNEP website] (https://www.unep.org/resources/report/marine-plastic-debris-and-microplastics-global-lessons-and-research-inspire-action-and)

3. Jambeck, J. R., Geyer, R., Wilcox, C., Siegler, T. R., Perryman, M., Andrady, A., ... & Law, K. L. (2015). Plastic waste inputs from land into the ocean. Science, 347(6223), 768–771. [DOI:

10.1126/science.1260352]

(https://doi.org/10.1126/science.1260352)

4. Hoornweg, D., & Bhada-Tata, P. (2012). What a waste: A global review of solid waste management. Urban Development Series Knowledge Papers No. 15. World Bank. [World Bank website] (https://openknowledge.worldbank.org/handle/10986/17388)

5. Secretariat of the Pacific Regional Environment Programme (SPREP). (2019). Baseline Report on the State of Marine Plastic Pollution in the Pacific Region. Apia, Samoa: SPREP. [SPREP website] (https://www.sprep.org/publications/baseline-report-on-the-state-of-marine-plastic-pollution-in-the-pacific-region)

6. United Nations. (2017). Resolution adopted by the General Assembly on 6 July 2017, Work of the Statistical Commission pertaining to the

2030 Agenda for Sustainable Development. A/RES/71/313. [UN website] (https://undocs.org/A/RES/71/313)

7. United Nations Economic and Social Commission for Asia and the Pacific (UNESCAP). (2019). Turning the Tide on Plastic Pollution in Asia and the Pacific. Bangkok, Thailand: UNESCAP. [UNESCAP website] (https://www.unescap.org/publications/turning-tide-plastic-pollution-asia-and-pacific)

8. International Union for Conservation of Nature (IUCN). (2018). Marine Plastic Pollution: An urgent need for action. Gland, Switzerland: IUCN. [IUCN website] (https://www.iucn.org/resources/issues-briefs/marine-plastic-pollution)

9. Global Environment Facility (GEF). (2019). Eliminating plastic pollution: A new GEF-funded project takes on marine plastics in Pacific Island Countries. [GEF website]

(https://www.thegef.org/news/eliminating-plastic-pollution-new-gef-funded-project-takes-marine-plastics-pacific-island)

10. Commonwealth Secretariat. (2018). Plastic Pollution in the Commonwealth: An Urgent Call for Action. London, UK: Commonwealth Secretariat. [Commonwealth Secretariat website] (https://thecommonwealth.org/sites/default/files/inline/Commonwealth%20Plastic%20Pollution%20Report.pdf)

11. Ocean Conservancy. (2020). Trash Free Seas Alliance: Strategies for a Plastic Free Ocean. [Ocean Conservancy website] (https://oceanconservancy.org/trash-free-seas/plastics-in-the-ocean/)

12. Rochman, C. M., Browne, M. A., Halpern, B. S., Hentschel, B. T., Hoh, E., Karapanagioti, H. K., ... & Thompson, R. C. (2013). Policy: Classify plastic waste as hazardous. Nature, 494(7436), 169–171.

[DOI: 10.1038/494169a] (https://doi.org/10.1038/494169a)

13. Smith, M., Love, D. C., Rochman, C. M., & Neff, R. A. (2018). Microplastics in seafood and the implications for human health. Current Environmental Health Reports, 5(3), 375–386. [DOI: 10.1007/s40572-018-0206-z] (https://doi.org/10.1007/s40572-018-0206-z)

14. World Bank. (2020). World Development Indicators database. [World Bank website] (https://databank.worldbank.org/source/world-development-indicators)

15. United Nations Development Programme (UNDP). (2019). Human Development Report 2019: Beyond income, beyond averages, beyond today: Inequalities in human development in the 21st century. New York, NY: UNDP. [UNDP website] (http://hdr.undp.org/en/2019-report)

16. Cesar, H. S. J., & Chircop, A. (2010). Marine pollution in small island developing states. Springer Science & Business Media. [Publisher's website] (https://www.springer.com/gp/book/9789048188917)

17. Secretariat of the Convention on Biological Diversity (CBD). (2012). Marine Debris and Plastic Pollution. Montreal, Canada: CBD. [CBD website] (https://www.cbd.int/doc/publications/cbd-ts-67-en.pdf)

18. United Nations Conference on Trade and Development (UNCTAD). (2018). Rethinking Plastics: Circular Economy Solutions to Marine Litter. Geneva, Switzerland: UNCTAD. [UNCTAD website] (https://unctad.org/system/files/official-document/ditcted2019d3_en.pdf)

19. Greenpeace. (2020). Plastic Free Islands: A roadmap towards islands free from plastic pollution. [Greenpeace website] (https://www.greenpeace.org/static/planet4-international-stateless/2019/07/6d9bda23-plastic-free-islands-roadmap-report-1.pdf)

20. Ellen MacArthur Foundation. (2016). The New Plastics Economy: Rethinking the future of plastics. Cowes, UK: Ellen MacArthur Foundation. [Ellen MacArthur Foundation website] (https://www.ellenmacarthurfoundation.org/publications/the-new-plastics-economy-rethinking-the-future-of-plastics)

This comprehensive list of references encompasses a wide range of sources, from scientific studies and reports to publications by international organizations and NGOs, providing a solid foundation of knowledge and research on the topic of plastic pollution in Small Island Developing States.

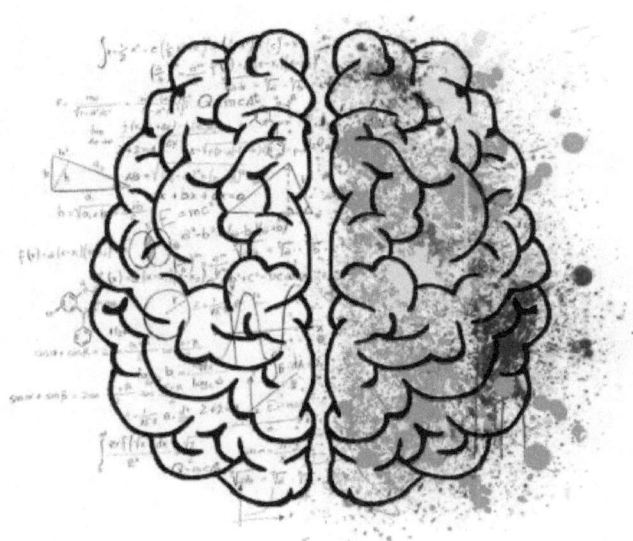

Further Reading

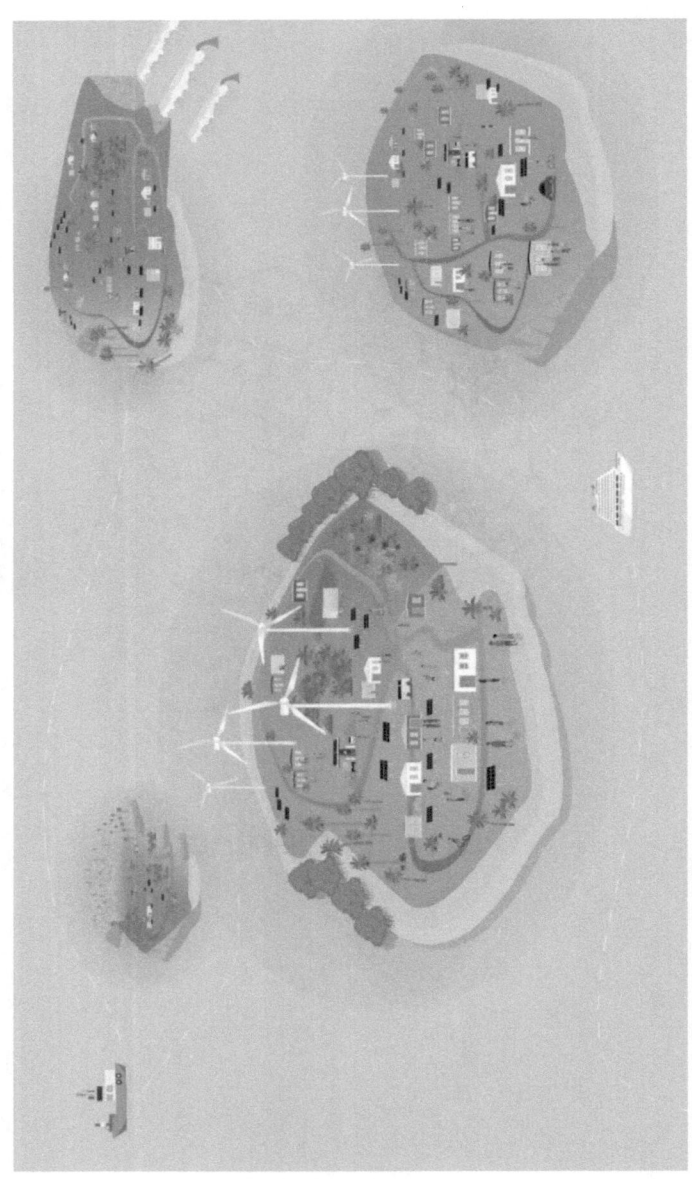

The journey towards mitigating plastic pollution in Small Island Developing States (SIDS) is multifaceted and requires ongoing learning and collaboration. This chapter provides a curated list of resources for readers who wish to delve deeper into the topics covered in this book, explore additional perspectives, and stay informed about the latest developments in the field.

1. Books

- Plastic-Free: How I Kicked the Plastic Habit and How You Can Too by Beth Terry

- The Story of Stuff: How Our Obsession with Stuff Is Trashing the Planet, Our Communities, and Our Health–and a Vision for Change by Annie Leonard

- Plastic Ocean: How a Sea Captain's Chance Discovery Launched a Determined Quest to Save the Oceans by Charles Moore and Cassandra Phillips

- No Impact Man: The Adventures of a Guilty Liberal Who Attempts to Save the Planet, and the Discoveries He Makes About Himself and Our Way of Life in the Process by Colin Beavan

2. Reports and Publications

- United Nations Environment Programme (UNEP) reports on marine plastic pollution and sustainable waste management practices in SIDS.

- World Bank publications on the economic impacts of plastic pollution and strategies for building resilience in coastal communities.

- Intergovernmental Panel on Climate Change (IPCC) assessments addressing the intersection of climate change, ocean health, and plastic pollution.

3. Academic Journals

- Marine Pollution Bulletin
- Environmental Science & Technology

- Frontiers in Marine Science
- Journal of Environmental Management

4. Websites and Online Resources

- The Ocean Cleanup (https://theoceancleanup.com/)
- Plastic Pollution Coalition (https://www.plasticpollutioncoalition.org/)
- Global Ocean Observing System (GOOS) Plastic Task Team (https://www.goosocean.org/index.php?option=com_content&view=article&id=114&Itemid=141)

5. Documentaries and Films

- A Plastic Ocean (2016)
- The Story of Plastic (2020)
- Bag It: Is Your Life Too Plastic? (2010)
- Albatross (2017)

6. Online Courses and Webinars

- Coursera: "Sustainable Waste Management: Solutions for a Changing Climate" (offered by the University of Queensland)

- edX: "Plastic Pollution: Challenges and Solutions" (offered by Wageningen University & Research)

7. Community Organizations and Initiatives

- Surfrider Foundation (https://www.surfrider.org/)

- 5 Gyres (https://www.5gyres.org/)

- Parley for the Oceans (https://www.parley.tv/)

8. Government and NGO Reports

- Reports and publications from relevant government agencies and non-governmental organizations working on environmental conservation, waste management, and sustainable development in SIDS.

By exploring these resources, readers can deepen their understanding of plastic pollution issues in SIDS, gain insights into effective mitigation strategies, and connect with a global community dedicated to preserving the health and resilience of our oceans. Together, we can turn the tide on plastic pollution and create a more sustainable future for all.

This chapter aims to provide readers with a comprehensive roadmap for further exploration and engagement in the crucial effort to mitigate plastic pollution in Small Island Developing States.

Notes

Notes

www.ingramcontent.com/pod-product-compliance
Lightning Source LLC
LaVergne TN
LVHW041908070526
838199LV00051BA/2542